Festa del Giardino

A harvest of recipes and family memories

SALLY MARAVENTANO

To Marsha,
Thank you for taking
such good care of us.
Enjoy the recipes
and the memories.
Buona Cucina!
Sally Maraventano
Oct. 3, 2018

Cover and Illustrations by Caterina Linarelli

FORUM ITALICUM

Dedication

In loving memory of my mother, Frances LoCascio Maraventano, my teacher and my friend.

And in loving memory of my grandparents, Giuseppina and Antonio LoCascio, who first taught me to treasure the fruits of the earth.

FORUM ITALICUM

Maraventano, Sally
  Festa del Giardino / Sally Maraventano.
    A harvest of recipes and family memories
    125 Italian vegetable recipes
  Includes index.
  ISBN 1-893127-99-0

Library of Congress Catalog Card Number: 99-93795

Cover and interior graphic design by Propeller Works
Illustrations ©1999 by Caterina Linarelli
Recipe format design by Jaime Robles

Printed in the United States of America

SINGLE COPIES MAY BE ORDERED FROM:

Cucina Casalinga
PO Box 7714
Wilton, CT 06897-7714
Phone/Fax (203) 762-0768
E-mail cucinacasa@aol.com
www.cucinacasalinga.com

Forum Italicum
Center for Italian Studies
State University of New York at Stony Brook
Stony Brook, NY 11794-3358
(516) 632-7444

Table of Contents

Acknowledgments

Festa del Giardino, my Italian vegetable cookbook, was inspired by the lives and traditions of my immigrant Sicilian grandparents and parents. They were a great influence on me and my passion for Italian cuisine.

And it is an honor for me that the Center for Italian Studies at the State University of New York at Stony Brook is publishing this, my "Feast from the Garden". Heartfelt thanks to Dr. Mario B. Mignone, Editor of the Forum Italicum and Director of the Center for Italian Studies. Millie grazie to Donna Severino and Kim Garvin for cheerfully researching the answers to my many questions; to Maria - Chiara Fabbian, who reviewed the Italian words and phrases used in the manuscript, and to my cousin Jo Fusco, Executive Director of the Center for Italian Studies, for nurturing and promoting my desire to share our family's rich heritage and love for Italian cuisine and culture.

Writing this cookbook would not have been possible without the support and help of many caring people; my long-time friend Miriam Luck convinced me almost 18 years ago to open my Italian cooking school, Cucina Casalinga. She has been with me since the beginning of this project, cheerfully transforming my recipes and notes into a cohesive manuscript. I thank also Jeremy Capocci for keeping this book "on line" through his computer wizardry!

For the artistic interpretation of *Festa del Giardino* I thank my friend and illustrator Caterina Linarelli Hammack. We have shared our love for our Italian heritage here and in Italy, and our desire to share this warm culture with others.

My loving father-in-law, Earl Kirmser contributed his knowledge and respect for the English language in editing my prose. Thank you, Dad.

I owe special thanks to the creative design services of Propeller Works: to Regina Vorgang and Denise Arsenault, my enthusiastic and most professional graphic artists, who also design my newsletter, to Scott Miles for the photography of the art work and my grandparents' heirloom photograph; to Geoff Parker of Valley Color Graphics for his technical assistance.

My thanks also to Jeanne Fredericks for suggesting years ago that I write a cookbook, to Leslie Yarborough for editing my manuscript, to Susan Silva for her enthusiasm and constant support; to Melanie Barnard for her friendship and encouragement.

My deepest appreciation to all of the talented chefs of Italy who have graciously shared *la vera cucina Italiana* with me and my students: Chef Enrico Franzese and Rosemary Anastasio, of the Luna Convento Cooking School in Amalfi; Peggy Markel and Chef Piero Ferrini of La Cucina Al Focolare in Reggello, Tuscany; Rolando Beramendi, founder of the Avignonesi Wine and Food Workshops in Tuscany; Antonio Sersale and Chef Alfonso Mazzacano of the Sirenuse Hotel, Positano; and Marchesa Anna Tasca Lanza for sharing her World of Regaleali with me and my family, and helping us discover our Sicilian roots.

Friends, students and family members enthusiastically contributed or tested recipes. Special thanks to Aunt Edith LoCascio Constantino, Mary Kimberlin, Balbina Schiano, Penny Brewer, Annie Kropp and Susan Mathews.

Special appreciation to Sal Gilbertie for his friendship and for sharing his knowledge of herbs with me; to my friends Ina Chadwick and Laurie Greene for assisting me in the final phase of the project.

Finally, thanks to my family for love, patience and support. I am grateful to my husband Ralph for encouraging me to write this book, for loving all things Italian as much as I do, and for his bountiful garden — the source of many wonderful vegetable recipes. My daughter Fran and sons Joe and Tony offered love, marketing suggestions, taste-testing and constant reassurance. Thank you, dear ones, for your love and for sharing our home with all those who come to cook with me.

Growing Up Italian

$\mathcal{M}$Y KITCHEN IS A COZY PLACE, fragrant with just-baked rosemary *focaccia* and a large tureen of *minestrone al pesto*. Multicolored plates from my culinary tours to Amalfi, Tuscany, and Sicily decorate my walls, and baskets laden with fresh vegetables adorn my counters. Above my window, a ceramic plaque given to me by a friend reads, "This Kitchen is Seasoned with Love."

Here, in my private world, I cook for my husband and our three children—and on holidays for my three sisters and their families, my husband's family, and our friends. Here, for 17 years, I have taught hundreds of women, men, and children the art of regional Italian cooking in my cooking school, *Cucina Casalinga*. *Cucina Casalinga* means "homestyle cooking—cooking with mother." I chose that name because it best describes how I learned to cook, beginning at the age of nine, with my mother and her father, Grandpa Tony LoCascio, a retired baker who emigrated to America from Catania, Sicily. In this special place, I share with my students the memories and stories of my Italian culinary heritage, and my philosophy on food and the table and its relationship to a happy family.

For Italians especially, the family dinner table evokes strong and, I believe, universal images. Professor August Coppola, in a recent documentary on "Little Italy," spoke of the ritual of the meal and of the table as a temple, with the grandparents at the head of the table, surrounded by children, grandchildren, aunts, uncles, and their children, in a ceremony that hasn't changed for centuries.

We gathered every Sunday at Grandpa Tony and Grandma Peppina's house—often more than 20 of us. We were quite a noisy bunch, laughing and talking and, of course, eating. Grandpa would send one of the grandchildren to get the big gallon jug of wine. He would pour the wine. We would all say grace together. Then the *antipasti* plates would arrive.

The bounty of our table seemed endless: course after course of wonderful Sicilian dishes. The *primo piatto* (first course) was always pasta, often combined with fresh vegetables. The *secondo piatto* (main course) was usually a meat or fish dish accompanied by several *contorni* (vegetable side dishes). Then came the *insalata mista,* a simple salad of greens, cucumbers, and tomatoes with an oil-and-vinegar dressing. And finally came the *dolci* (desserts): *frutta fresca* (fresh fruit) always preceded something sweet and wonderful, such as a tray of my mother's *biscotti* (cookies) or Aunt Yolanda's *torta di ricotta* (ricotta cheesecake). Finishing the meal was strong, piping-hot espresso!

Through all the courses, conversation never lagged—about politics, religion, opera, sports, news of friends, school events, vacation plans. Jokes were told and ideas exchanged in various degrees of loudness. A sense of well-being filled the dining room. The food was served slowly, in order to be savored.

Surrounded by food and family on these Sunday afternoons, we established—through my grandparents' stories—who we were and would become as Italian-Americans. The spirit of our heritage was expressed in the traditional foods we ate at those special family dinners.

My father, Salvatore Maraventano, was born in Agrigento, Sicily. As a young boy, he emigrated to the United States with his parents and five brothers and sisters, settling in New York in the Arthur Avenue section of the Bronx, the same neighborhood where my mother's family lived and where he would later practice medicine.

My father died at an early age when I was seven years old. My mother was left to raise four young daughters. Our lives changed; the close-knit association with my grandparents, aunts, and uncles tightened as they became involved in our daily lives in order to lend emotional and physical support to my mother, my sisters, and me. Mom started her own gift basket business in our home, and Grandpa Tony stayed with us for weeks at a time. He assumed the role of family shopper and cook—and he was a fantastic cook! As a child, I loved to stand near him and watch as he worked his magic in the kitchen. He was also a consummate gardener.

When I reflect on my relationship to the fruits of the earth, I vividly recall a scene from my early childhood: I was standing in the late-afternoon summer sun, in our tiny, sandy alley garden at our beach cottage on Long Island, and I was biting into a ripe, red, juicy plum tomato, newly plucked from the vine. My sister, Frani, and I, five and six years old, were having our ritual afternoon snack, having just showered and changed into clean pinafores after a day on the beach. While other children were probably eating ice cream cones, Grandpa Tony's tomatoes beckoned to us.

This *piccolo giardino* (little garden) was a miniature version of the large plot he cultivated at his home on the south shore of Long Island. There he grew watermelons, pumpkins, and many varieties of tomatoes, basil, squash, eggplants, string beans, Swiss chard, fennel, and other fresh vegetables that formed the basis of our daily diet. His fig tree endures today, 28 years after his death.

As I grew older, I became my mother's assistant in the kitchen. This evolved into a culinary partnership that strengthened and grew until she died in 1993. Even though she had the responsibility of her business, she enjoyed preparing family meals. I learned from Mom that cooking is fun and relaxing; it is a creative expression of our caring for those who would share the table with us. She called cooking a "labor of love." Mom and I often laughed over a lunchtime sandwich as we caught ourselves passionately discussing what delights we were going to prepare for dinner! We spoke of our ingredients in personal terms: "You take your broccoli and separate it into florets while I peel my garlic."

Perhaps the greatest lesson I learned from my mother was that cooking is an art. The diverse but simple methods used by Italians in preparing seasonal fresh vegetables confirm that lesson. The basic secret of Italian vegetable preparation is simple: combine just-picked vegetables with an aromatic flavoring of olive oil, garlic, and herbs. The presentation of a variety of fresh vegetables, with all their splendid colors, combined in a savory soup, sauce, or baked dish is a feast for the eyes as well as the palate.

VEGETABLES ITALIAN-STYLE

It is interesting that there is no vegetarian movement in Italy. To the Italians, a day—in fact, a lunch or dinner—without *verdure* (vegetables) would be a near-tragedy! In a country where the landscape and climate foster the cultivation of a wide variety of vegetables, it is taken for granted that vegetables will always take center stage on the table.

For centuries, many Italians lived on *la cucina povera,* a diet based primarily on vegetables, eggs, and cheese, with bread as a constant at every meal. Meat was at a premium in many parts of Italy because of the mountainous terrain and a lack of pastureland on most of the mainland and the islands. Fish was a more typical main course, as well as pork and young animal meats such as veal, lamb, and goat, although these dishes were more apt to be found on the tables of the wealthy and noble families.

Today, when economic restraints are not such a great factor, the love affair with vegetables—whether alone, in combination with pasta, risotto, and polenta, or in soups and stews—is shared by Italians of all economic levels alike. My mother and I often found it amusing that our favorite peasant dish—escarole and beans—has become "chic" in the United States in the last 10 to 15 years. Americans are finally realizing what Italians have known for centuries: that vegetables are the greatest!

Whether simply sautéed with extra-virgin olive oil and garlic, or cooked for hours with beans and grains, vegetables always promote good health and provide a feeling of satisfaction. The use of olive oil, and in particular extra-virgin olive oil, in the recipes in this book is a departure from the *pancetta* (bacon) and meat bases used in traditional non-vegetarian Italian cooking. Medical research shows that olive oil has one of the highest levels of mono-unsaturated fats found in any food; it may lower the level of LDL ("bad cholesterol"), and could even raise the level of HDL ("good cholesterol"), in a person's blood. These factors support the use of olive oil in everyday cooking, and its marvelous flavor is a bonus. Most of these recipes use just a few tablespoons of olive oil to enhance the preparation of the fresh vegetables, but for people who are watching their fat intake, smaller amounts of oil may be used; a little goes a long way.

Festa del Giardino features a wide variety of vegetable recipes that I hope will satisfy vegetarians and non-vegetarians alike. Strict vegetarians will enjoy the recipes that pair favorite vegetables with the little-known but ancient grain *farro*, with *arborio* rice and pasta, and with the exotic addition of raisins and pinoli (pine nuts), sugar and vinegar, and a variety of fresh herbs. For those who want to expand their meatless-entree repertoire, I have included hearty dishes containing fillings of the rich cheeses the Italians love so much. The chapters on soups and pasta dishes will help those cooking on a budget who want to provide flavorful yet inexpensive meals for themselves and their families.

Most of the recipes in this book are easy to prepare and can be made in a short time, or prepared ahead and frozen for those busy days when schedules and children's activities seem to rob us of the sacred dinner hour. With a little long-range planning, nutritious vegetable meals can be pulled from the freezer, warmed in the microwave or oven, and put on the table in just a few minutes.

I think of *Festa del Giardino* as an extension of my cooking school. It is an opportunity to share my family's traditions and recipes with readers who are too far away to cook with me in my home. I hope the warmth that I feel as I cook with my students will come through in every vegetable recipe in this book. *Buona Cucina!*

The Italian Pantry

M Y FATHER USED TO SAY, "A rich man can eat from his pantry for seven days." I have thought of his words many times while preparing countless meals for my family using ingredients always on my pantry shelves, in the refrigerator, and in the freezer.

After a series of vacation meals in restaurants, nothing is more delicious than spaghetti with *marinara* sauce, or "quick sauce," as we call it in our house. Canned tomatoes with *cannellini* or *ceci* beans make a healthful, quick pasta-and-soup dish when cooked with extra-virgin olive oil, garlic, and rosemary.

The possibilities for quick, nutritious pantry-inspired meals are endless. This chapter lists the fresh and dry (pantry) ingredients most important in Italian vegetarian cooking. I have divided these ingredients into several sections: The Pantry Shelf, Olives, Olive Oil, Cheeses, The Italian Herb Garden, and The Kitchen Garden.

DRY GOODS

Beans *(fagioli):* dried and canned beans, including *cannellini, ceci* (chick peas), *borlotti,* and *fava*

Cornmeal *(polenta):* coarse-grained cornmeal imported from Italy

Farro: an ancient grain, often called "spelt," used in a variety of ways in its whole-grain state (see *Insalata di Farro,* page 46) and crushed for use in soups or in a *risotto*-like dish called *Farrotto con Peperoni* (see page 117)

Flour *(farina):* all-purpose, unbleached

Lentils *(lenticchie):* dried, for use in soups and salads

Salt *(sale):* including sea salt (both fine and coarse-grain), for its rich mineral content and fine flavor

Semolina flour: flour made from the hard durum wheat and used in bread baking (especially Sicilian), for pizza dough, and for *Gnocchi alla Romana* (page 122)

Pasta: imported from Italy, dry varieties (long and short) (see Chapter 6)

Rice *(riso):* imported from Italy, several varieties *(arborio, carnaroli,* and *vialone nano)* are used in making *risotto* (see Chapter 7)

Yeast *(lievito):* leavening agent for dough (see Chapter 8)

CANNED AND BOTTLED INGREDIENTS

Anchovies *(acciughe):* optional, but a key ingredient in many Sicilian vegetable recipes

Anise oil, vanilla, cinnamon, and other flavorings for baking

Bread crumbs *(pane grattugiato):* fine, dried, unseasoned

Capers *(capperi):* in brine or packed in salt

Coffee *(caffè):* espresso

Dried herbs: including oregano *(origano),* thyme *(timo),* bay leaves *(alloro),* and rosemary *(rosmarino)*

Extra-virgin olive oil *(olio extra-vergine di oliva):* also olive oil (see page 12 for a description of the different types of olive oil) and vegetable oil (for deep frying)

Olives *(olive):* bottled, imported, for use only when fresh olives are not available

Pine nuts *(pinoli),* as well as hazelnuts, almonds and sesame seeds

Porcini mushrooms *(funghi secchi porcini):* dried, imported from Italy

Sugar *(zucchero):* granulated and confectioner's for baking

Sultana raisins (golden) *(uvetta):* used often in Neapolitan and Sicilian dishes

Tomatoes *(pomodori):* whole plum tomatoes, canned in their juices; crushed, recipe-ready plum tomatoes; and, if possible, canned cherry tomatoes (from San Marzano on the Amalfi coast) and boxed Pomi tomatoes (crushed or strained)

Tomato paste *(concentrato or estratto di pomodoro):* in tubes or small cans

Vinegar *(aceto):* red wine vinegar and a good-quality, aged, imported balsamic vinegar from Modena, Italy

Bottled spring water: for bread and other recipes when the quality and taste of tap water is questionable

Wine *(vino):* a variety of red and white wines, imported from all of the regions of Italy

OLIVES

Olive trees have graced the landscape of Italy for thousands of years, and olives have enhanced the flavor and texture of Italian cuisine all that time.

Olives are black or green, depending on when they are harvested. An olive on the tree changes from green, to purple or brown, to black. Just picked from the tree, olives taste bitter—nothing like those we enjoy at the table. It is in the curing process that each olive develops its own unique flavor. Some olives are preserved in oil, others in salt brine, and still others simply dried. The texture of a good olive, no matter what variety, should be firm, never mushy. While inhabitants of some Mediterranean countries eat olives only uncooked (i.e., cured or marinated), Italians use them in combination with many other foods. The blending of black, tangy olives with fresh tomatoes, garlic, and extra-virgin olive oil results in a rich, spicy sauce for pasta *Linguine alla Bella Donna* (page 87).

I will list here some of the types of olives you will find in good Italian specialty shops, and some varieties that are available in your local markets.

Black olives: *Gaeta* (small), Greek *Kalamata* (long and pointed), dry-cured Sicilian (small), *Itrana* (small)

Green olives: *Ascolana* (large and slightly oval), *Castelvetrano* (small green), *Ceriniola Barese* (very large), Sicilian (very large: 1 1/2 inches in diameter)

Olives should be served at room temperature and may be stored covered with olive oil in a glass jar in a cool place. To pit olives, use a heavy mallet (I use a meat tenderizer with a flat bottom) and place olives in one layer on a cutting board covered with paper toweling. Hit each olive with a mallet then squeeze the pit out. Small olives like the *Gaeta* variety should be tapped lightly until cracked; the pits will slip out easily.

EXTRA-VIRGIN OLIVE OIL

Extra-virgin olive oil is so important to the preparation of these vegetarian dishes that I'd like to provide some information about it, especially about how it is made and how to identify the best varieties.

In Italy, olives are harvested by hand, using plastic or wooden rakes to release the olives from the trees without damaging or pulling off the leaves. Large nets are often spread under the trees to catch the fruit as it falls. The olives are then rushed to the mills for same-day or next-day pressing by mechanical stainless-steel grindstones. The paste that results is pressed on circular hemp mats, squeezing out the liquid from the olives. This oil is not altered by chemical additives and it contains no more than 1% of free oleic acid. Only olive oil containing less than 1% of oleic acid qualifies as extra-virgin. The lower the free oleic-acid content, the higher the quality of olive oil.

The olives are harvested beginning in October and for three to four months after. In Tuscany, olives are usually picked while they are very green and before the danger of heavy frost. The extra-virgin olive oil made from these under-ripe olives is usually an intense green color and produces a peppery sensation at the back of your throat after you swallow. Oil made from riper Ligurian olives is more yellow, with a more delicate buttery flavor.

Excellent extra-virgin olive oils are bottled within a month or two of pressing and are best consumed in the year after they are bottled, but they will remain in good condition for up to two years. Store bottled olive oil (dark bottles keep better) in a cool, dark place away from direct sunlight. Estate-bottled extra-virgin olive oils are usually of superior quality and typically have the date of production on the label.

Here are a few brands of select extra-virgin olive oils and the regions from which they come: *Rustichella* (Abruzzo), *Masserie di Sant'Eramo* (Apuglia), *Ceppo Antico* (Liguria), *Fini* and *Lungarotti* (Umbria), *Laudemio, Castello di Ama, Capezzana* (Tuscany), and *Olio Verde* (Sicily). Use extra virgin olive oil when intense "stand alone" flavor is desired such as, on salads, vegetables, with bread for dipping, or as a final addition to soup before serving.

OTHER TYPES OF OLIVE OIL

Virgin olive oil: oil obtained by mechanical methods from the fruit of the olive tree, which has good color, aroma, and flavor, but not to the exacting standards of extra virgin.

Olive oil: virgin olive oil that does not meet the criteria for extra virgin in terms of color, flavor, or aroma is refined to a neutral state and blended with between 5% and 25% unrefined virgin olive oil. Marketed as "olive oil" (formerly called "pure olive oil"). Use for general-purpose cooking, in sauces, or marinades.

CHEESES (*FORMAGGI*)

Cheese has long been a nutritious part of the Italian diet. The many varieties produced in Italy are largely a result of the diverse geography of this long and mountainous country. From the lush green countryside of Lombardy in the north, and its rich cow's milk, come cheeses like *Gorgonzola* and *Taleggio;* harder *Asiago* comes from the Veneto, and the world-renowned *Parmigiano-Reggiano* is made in Emilia-Romagna. The hilly central regions of Abruzzo, Lazio, and Campania are famous for cheeses formed from curds, such as *Mozzarella di Bufala* and

Scamorza, as well as cheeses made from the milk of *pecora* (sheep) and *capra* (goat). The islands of Sicily and Sardinia are noted for their sheep's-milk cheeses, such as *Pecorino* and the versatile *Ricotta,* used both in stuffed pastas and *dolci* (dessert) fillings.

The cheeses used in the recipes in this book are listed below:

Bel Paese: a semi-soft mild and creamy cheese. It can sometimes be substituted in recipes that call for mozzarella, and is also delicious served after dinner with fresh fruit.

Caciocavallo ("cheese on horseback"): cow's-milk cheese produced in almost every region of southern Italy. White and even-textured inside, mild when young and stronger as it ages, this cheese derives its name from its flask-like shape, tied tightly at the top and hung by strings over a pole to mature.

Fontina: a typical cheese of the Val d'Aosta, made from whole cow's milk. It has a thin, rather russet-colored rind, is quite soft, and is pale to deep straw-colored inside. A good table cheese, it is also used in cooking.

Mascarpone: a spreading cheese that looks like very thick cream. It is used in delicate pasta dishes in place of butter or cream, in desserts as a topping for fresh berries, and as part of the filling for the famous *Tiramisù.* It is highly perishable.

Mozzarella: the most famous variety, *mozzarella di bufala,* is made from buffalo's milk in the region of Campania (Naples). More readily available and more reasonable in price is the whole-milk mozzarella made from cow's milk. It is best eaten fresh, but in the United States it is most often used as a topping for pizza.

Parmigiano-Reggiano: the "King of Cheeses," this is the ultimate choice to serve freshly grated over most pasta dishes. Production of this cheese is strictly regulated as to the area where it can be made (Emilia-Romagna) and the time required for aging before the cheese can be sold (18 months at a minimum). It has a pale straw color with a rich texture and a slightly salty flavor, and can be broken into chunks. The authentic *Parmigiano-Reggiano* has its name deeply embossed on the rind. It is one of the most delicious table cheeses, eaten in chunks or sliced paper-thin and served on *crostini*.

Pecorino Romano: very popular in the United States, this white, dense, sharp-tasting cheese is made exclusively from sheep's milk.

Pecorino Sardo and *Pecorino Siciliano:* these are other versions of *pecorino*, made with whole sheep's milk and produced locally on the two largest islands off the mainland of Italy. *Pecorino Sardo* is formed in cone-shaped molds, and *Pecorino Siciliano* is shaped in wicker molds (basket cheese).

Provolone: made with whole cow's milk, it can be produced in many shapes—some formed like *Caciocavallo,* others cone-shaped, round like melons, or long like sausages. *Provolone* is white or pale-straw-colored and is sold in three varieties: mild, strong, and smoked. It makes a delicious table cheese when served with crusty Italian bread.

Ricotta: a soft, unsalted sheep's-milk cheese, which should be eaten very fresh. Seasoned with salt and pepper and mixed with other ingredients, it is often used as a stuffing for pasta. When sweetened, it is used in pies, cakes, and pastries.

Ricotta salata: from Sicily, it is semi-salty and semi-hard; when aged it can be grated (see *Rigatoni alla Norma,* page 98).

Scamorza: from the region of *Calabria* and *Apulia,* this is a melting cheese used in recipes such as *Mozzarella in Carrozza* (mozzarella in a carriage), which is a deep-fried cheese sandwich.

THE ITALIAN HERB GARDEN

Sal Gilbertie is a well-known commercial herb grower in Westport, Connecticut. He and his wife, Marie, are special friends of mine and they enjoyed experiencing the herbs of Italy on one of our culinary tours to Tuscany. On the beautiful fifteenth-century estate of *La Fattoria degli Usignoli* (the Farm of the Nightingales), we reveled in the sight of rosemary hedges bordering the length of the swimming pool, huge bushes of bay leaves, and wild fennel growing amid the olive and fig trees. Mint, sage, basil, parsley, thyme, and oregano grew in profusion on the ground and in the many enormous terra cotta planters.

Like Sal's grandmother, my grandfather never had a formal herb garden. All the fragrant herbs mentioned above grew amid his tomato plants, eggplants, and other *verdure*. Your recipes will turn out especially tasty if you grow the herbs you use in your daily cooking. Your herb garden may be a large plot, or just a few containers on your deck or patio.

Following is a list of the herbs that I grow in my herb border close to the house, and others that my husband includes in his large vegetable garden:

Arugula *(rucola):* has a pungent, slightly bitter flavor, and gives a salad of mild greens a real boost. Arugula can also be sautéed with garlic, olive oil, and fresh plum tomatoes for a quick, light sauce for pasta.

Basil *(basilico):* is probably the most popular and widely used herb in Italian cooking, and is always used in combination with tomatoes. While there are dozens of varieties of basil, and many of them are available in American nurseries today, bush basil is the most common one grown for the home kitchen. Dwarf basil, grown in a globe-shaped bush, is great for growing in pots. A few good-sized basil plants will insure a supply of pesto sauce for the long winter ahead.

Fennel *(finocchio):* usually grows wild in Italy, and has a licorice flavor and the fernlike leaves have a feathery appearance much like that of dill. You will see it more often in Italy than in the United States. It is best known in the famous Sicilian dish, *Pasta con le Sarde*—an exotic mix of fresh sardines, wild fennel, currants, and pinoli nuts mixed with thin *maccheroncelli* pasta, baked in the oven and topped with toasted bread crumbs. The other fennel (Florence), with a white bulb and licorice flavor, is eaten raw with fruit and nuts or baked in the oven with Parmesan cheese. It is found in the produce sections of markets as "anise."

Garlic *(aglio):* long associated with Italian cooking, it also enjoys a reputation as a healing and preventive aid in many illnesses. The combination of garlic and extra-virgin olive oil raises the flavors of tender, fresh vegetables to new heights.

Mint *(menta):* a prolific perennial herb, not easily confined to a given space. We grow ours at the edge of my husband's vegetable garden, and it manages to escape beyond the barrier of the wire fence every year. Sicilians are particularly fond of mint used in combination with olive oil and vinegar as a dressing for fried zucchini, onions, long green peppers, and other fresh vegetables.

Nutmeg *(noce moscata):* common in ravioli dishes containing spinach and ricotta—freshly grated or ground in a mill is preferable to the pre-ground bottles sold in the store.

Oregano *(origano):* a perennial herb that grows in a low, spreading cluster. When buying starter plants, be careful to choose the right variety; it should have a sharp, pungent flavor like the one you experience on pizza. I dry the stems laden with tiny leaves, and use them more often in this state than fresh, as the flavor intensifies once the leaves have dried.

Parsley *(prezzemolo):* Italian flat-leaf parsley has more flavor than the decorative curly variety, and is the parsley of choice of Italian cooks. It is a hardy biennial herb and grows very easily in the garden.

Pepper *(pepe):* black ground pepper and crushed hot pepper flakes or whole dried chili peppers *(peperoncini).*

Rosemary *(rosmarino):* a lovely perennial that is easy to grow indoors in pots in winter. Rosemary produces a beautiful blue flower and is often trained into topiaries. Rosemary flavors hearty soups, especially those containing chickpeas (garbanzo beans), and is marvelous as a topping for the flat yeast bread *(focaccia)* so popular now in the United States.

Saffron *(zafferano):* used in many risotto dishes. It is very expensive and comes powdered in packets and in threads. Must be steeped in water or broth before adding to other ingredients.

Sage *(salvia):* a hardy perennial with greenish-gray leaves that have a strong, must-like scent.

Sweet marjoram *(maggiorana):* delicate, fragrant, and well suited to container planting, this versatile herb complements soups, egg dishes, salads, and many other vegetables.

Thyme *(timo):* a perennial of many varieties. Slightly pungent, it enhances the flavor of vegetable soups and ragù (sauces). The Tuscans use it in their famous vegetable soup, *Ribollita*, which utilizes stale Italian bread and a variety of vegetables and beans.

I am addicted to fresh herbs, and will go to great lengths and expense in winter to buy those that I cannot successfully grow in my sunny kitchen. I rarely use dry basil, as I find both the flavor and texture too far off from the real thing. Some people preserve basil leaves *sott'olio*, in a jar covered with olive oil. My cousin, Jo, freezes basil leaves in water in individual ice-cube trays to add to soups, stews, and tomato sauces. And many cooks process the fresh basil into a paste mixed with olive oil only (no cheese or garlic, as in pesto). Spoonfuls of this herb-oil mixture are added to dishes calling for fresh basil.

Finally, remember to use minced fresh herbs mixed with extra-virgin olive oil as a marinade before grilling eggplant, zucchini, peppers, onions, and all the wonderful fresh vegetables you grow in your home garden. These aromatic herb marinades and sauces are a great substitute for salt, especially when combined with freshly ground pepper.

THE KITCHEN GARDEN

On a recent Saturday morning, while testing recipes for this book, I asked my husband if he smelled the Swiss chard *torta* I was baking. He responded, "It smells wonderful—it smells like Italy!"

We had been reminiscing over our morning coffee about our trip last fall to Sicily and our walk through the *Vucciria,* the bustling open-air market in Palermo. We were in awe of the scene before us that day: the still-life quality of the rows and rows of vegetables, fruits, and nuts. It reminded me of a passage by D.H. Lawrence, describing a market stall at the end of a dark street:

"Abundance of vegetables—piles of white and green fennel, like celery, and great sheaves of young purplish, sea-dust-coloured artichokes . . . long strings of dried figs, mountains of big oranges, scarlet red peppers, a large slice of pumpkin, a great mass of colours and vegetable freshnesses . . ."

Here is a list of the vegetables most often used in the Italian kitchen. I begin with the vegetables found in a classic *battuto* or *soffritto:* a mixture of diced onions, garlic, carrots, and celery that is used as a base for hearty vegetable soups and *ragù* (sauces).

Onions *(cipolle):* the yellow sweet variety is used as a flavoring for soups, stews, and sauces. Tuscans most often use large red onions for *battuto;* in southern Italy, these magnificent sweet onions are used raw in tomato salad and in fennel and orange salad *Insalata di Finocchio con Arancia* (page 51). Other onions used in Italian cooking are scallions (green onions) and chives. Shallots are the most delicate of onions; they marry well with mushrooms, and can easily be grown in the home garden. Leeks, sweet and delicate, are used in many soups and sauces like *Brodo di Verdura* (page 61) (see "The Kitchen Garden," page 21).

Carrots *(carote):* used in vegetable soups and stews when mature, but also delicious when young—just two or three inches long—and simply sliced and sautéed with a few tablespoons of butter and dry Marsala wine, as the Sicilians do.

Celery *(sedano):* used in vegetable soups and stews, and in salads such as Aunt Edith's Sicilian Olive Salad (page 40). Stalks should be crisp and white, with few blemishes. The leaves are used in vegetable broths such as *Brodo di Verdura* (page 61) and in salads.

Artichokes *(carciofi):* thistle-like plants very popular in Italian cooking, with variations in preparation depending on the region: deep-fried in Rome, stuffed and stewed on the Amalfi coast, and combined with fresh fava beans and peas in Sicily. The artichoke is globular in shape, and the leaves should be tight and firm. The heart of the artichoke is the most tender and succulent part of the plant.

Asparagus *(asparagi):* one of the most versatile vegetables in Italian cuisine; featured in first-course *risotto*, pasta and soup dishes, as a *contorni* (side dish). Tips should be tight and stalks bright green. Stalks are usually scraped with a vegetable peeler and the tips rinsed well, before cooking.

Broccoli *(broccoli):* used in many Sicilian recipes, from soups and stews to pasta dishes and fillings for *calzone*. Rich in fiber. The flower clusters should be compact and firm, with the color ranging from dark green to purplish green. Wash thoroughly after separating into florets.

Broccoli Rabe *(broccoli di rape):* a member of the turnip family, this is quite bitter but delicious sautéed in extra virgin olive oil and garlic. Used in combination with pasta and also as a *contorni* or as a stuffing in calzone.

Cauliflower *(cavolfiore):* available year-round in the United States. Used in combination with pasta and in many *contorni* (side dishes). Florets should be tight and creamy-white, the outer leaves fresh and green.

Cucumbers *(cetrioli):* good in simple mixed salads and also in Panzanella.

Eggplant *(melanzane):* beloved in Sicilian cuisine, eggplant recipes have endless variations. Grown in many sizes and colors, the deep-purple variety is easily grown in home gardens and readily available in produce markets. Eggplants should feel very firm, with no bruises, cuts, or discolorations on the smooth skin. Regardless of the recipe, eggplant should be salted generously and weighted with a heavy object in a colander for at least 30 minutes, then rinsed and dried prior to frying, baking, or sautéeing, in order to eliminate the eggplant's bitter juices.

Mushrooms *(funghi):* used throughout Italy in many different ways, depending on the cuisine of the particular region. Large strong-flavored *porcini* mushrooms are popular in the north, while field mushrooms are used in recipes all over Italy, as in *Funghi Sott' Olio di Mamma* (page 39) and *Funghi al Forno* (page 187). Mushrooms should be wiped with a damp cloth, never washed or peeled unless absolutely necessary.

Potatoes *(patate):* used with great versatility in Italian cuisine: mashed in a pie *Gattò di Patate* (page 182), combined with flour and egg to form dumplings in dishes such as *Gnocchi alla Sorrentina* (page 120), and simply sliced and baked with extra-virgin olive oil and oregano in a very hot oven for *Patate Origanate* (page 189).

Radicchio: used primarily in salads in the United States, radicchio is treated as a *contorni* in Italy, where it is braised, grilled, and fried. The leaves are a variegated reddish-purplish and white color, and they grow in small, tight heads.

String beans *(fagiolini):* delicate and delicious when prepared simply with extra-virgin olive oil, garlic, and a sprinkling of fresh parsley. Also used in combination with pasta and pesto or in soups such as *Minestra di Fagiolini, Pomodoro e Patate* (page 71).

Peppers *(peperoni):* sweet, bell, red, yellow, orange, green, and Italian frying peppers are used in recipes throughout Italy. Fried, roasted, stewed, or stuffed—the possibilities are endless!

Peperoncini: small, hot chili peppers, used whole or dry and crushed.

Tomatoes *(pomodori):* especially popular in the cuisine of southern Italy. Technically a fruit, tomato is often eaten raw in salads. Plum tomatoes and other varieties are used in sauces for pasta and also in combination with other vegetables for *antipasti, contorni,* and main dishes. Tomatoes should be plump and red, and should have unblemished skins. To peel tomatoes plunge into boiling water for 30 seconds and then into ice water. The skins will peel easily. When serving tomatoes, think basil; the two go hand in hand!

Zucchini *(zucchine):* green and yellow varieties of summer squash, best used when young and tender; they become tough and seedy as they mature into long, large sizes. Used as *antipasti,* in *risotto* and pasta dishes, and sautéed, baked, or stuffed as a main course. Squash should be bright green or yellow, with a smooth skin and few blemishes. Carefully wash and scrub these vegetables before using, because typically, the skin is not peeled before using.

Cabbage *(cavolo):* used in vegetable soups and stews. Delicious combined with cheese and *arborio* rice in a *risotto*-like dish, *Riso e Verza* (page 72), featuring the Savoy variety of cabbage with ruffled leaves. Heads should be solid and heavy with little or no discoloration. Wash cabbage after shredding or chopping.

Leafy vegetables: spinach *(spinaci),* Swiss chard *(bietole),* and escarole *(scarola)* are leafy and green, and delicious sautéed in extra-virgin olive oil and garlic, or in soups such as *Zuppa di Scarola e Fagioli* (page 63) or *torte* such as *Torta di Bietole* (page 154). Leafy vegetables tend to be very gritty and need to be well washed in several changes of water.

Leeks *(porri):* long green stalk-like plants with a white bulb. I use these mildly onion-flavored herbs in delicate vegetable soups, and always in homemade vegetable broth. The one warning I offer concerns the leek's propensity to hold dirt and grit between its leaves: you must slit the leek in half lengthwise and rinse well between each layer before adding it to the pot.

Antipasti

RECIPES

- *Bruschetta al Pomodoro*
  GRILLED BREAD WITH TOMATO AND BASIL

- *Crostini di Verdure*
  LITTLE TOASTS WITH MUSHROOM VEGETABLE TOPPING
  (AND OTHER VARIATIONS)

- *Insalata Caprese*
  LAYERED FRESH MOZZARELLA AND TOMATOES WITH BASIL

- *Caponata*
  SICILIAN EGGPLANT RELISH

- *Carciofi Aglio e Olio alla Menta*
  TINY ARTICHOKES WITH EXTRA-VIRGIN OLIVE OIL,
  GARLIC, AND MINT

- *Melanzane e Zucchine alla Griglia*
  GRILLED EGGPLANT AND ZUCCHINI

- *Peperoni Arrostiti*
  ROASTED PEPPERS

- *Taglianelle alla Siciliana*
  MOM'S SICILIAN STUFFED GREEN FRYING PEPPERS

- *Zucchine a Scapecce*
  FRIED ZUCCHINI SLICES MARINATED IN EXTRA-VIRGIN
  OLIVE OIL, VINEGAR, AND FRESH MINT

- *Funghi Sott'Olio di Mamma*
  MOM'S MARINATED MUSHROOMS

- *Insalata di Olive in Marinata*
  AUNT EDITH'S SICILIAN OLIVE SALAD

*I*N ALMOST EVERY RESTAURANT in Italy, from the most elegant *ristorante* to the tiniest *trattoria*, the *antipasto* buffet is a constant. A myriad of colorful and beautifully displayed grilled, roasted, marinated, and fried fresh vegetables adorned the lavish buffet table at The Grand Hotel Villa Igiea in Palermo, Sicily, and at the charming La Piazetta Trattoria in the public square in Taormina. Italians today expect a variety of fresh *antipasti* dishes to start off their meal properly.

Americans are learning to appreciate and to prepare these varied and tasty dishes. Because of the variety of vegetables and salads in the category of *antipasti*, several of these dishes are often served as an entire luncheon or light supper menu, with the addition of a crusty loaf of Italian bread or an herbed *focaccia* (flat bread). Any of these *antipasti* recipes could also be served as a *contorno* (side dish) to accompany the main course.

The key element in the preparation of *antipasti* dishes is the quality of the produce; use the freshest vegetables and the ripest tomatoes available. The second essential ingredient in any vegetable *antipasto* is a good-quality extra-virgin olive oil. The true flavors of fresh, vine-ripened tomatoes, grilled eggplant, roasted peppers, marinated zucchini, mushrooms, and olives shine through only with the addition of extra-virgin olive oil.

Besides *antipasto's* usual role as part of a family meal, an *antipasto* party is a fabulous way to entertain, and is very satisfying from a culinary and decorative perspective. On one of my culinary tours to Italy, I found an *antipastiera*—a set of six fluted serving dishes surrounding a large platter—painted in the center in the Raffaelesco Renaissance pattern of Deruta: twin dragons in vibrant blues, golds, greens, and reds on a white background. The side dishes fit around the platter like the pieces of a puzzle—a breathtaking sight when filled with multicolored roasted peppers, marinated fresh artichokes, layered mozzarella and sliced ripe tomatoes garnished with fresh basil leaves, succulent black and green olives, grilled eggplant and zucchini, and stuffed green frying peppers. On the center platter are *bruschette* (grilled bread brushed with olive oil) and *crostini* (small toasts) with a variety of toppings.

This chapter invites you to try the delectable *antipasti* dishes I have described. The selection is a sampling; there are dozens of vegetable recipes suitable for *antipasti*.

I can't think of a healthier, more exciting way to start a meal than with a variety of vegetable *antipasti*. One of the best features of *antipasti* recipes is that you can make them in advance, allowing the flavors to blend and intensify. Only the final drizzling of extra-virgin olive oil and a sprinkling of fresh herbs should be left to the last minute. Arrange the vegetables on attractive platters and serve at room temperature. *Buon appetito!*

• In Tuscany *Bruschetta,* or *Fettunta,* is a thick slice of bread grilled on an open fire, then brushed with a peppery extra-virgin olive oil and a rubbing of garlic. It is heavenly in its simplicity. Spread with a topping of fresh tomatoes, basil, and extra-virgin olive oil, it is often presented at the table in restaurants throughout Italy as a complimentary appetizer even before the diner orders from the menu.

^{1}/$_{2}$ cup of extra-virgin olive oil
4 to 5 leaves of fresh basil, torn
^{1}/$_{4}$ red onion, finely diced (optional)
1 teaspoon of dried oregano
salt and freshly ground pepper to taste
1 ^{1}/$_{2}$ pounds of ripe tomatoes, diced but not peeled
1 loaf of crusty Italian bread, sliced ^{1}/$_{2}$ inch thick
2 to 3 cloves of garlic, sliced in half

1. Combine ^{1}/$_{4}$ cup of the olive oil with basil, a sprinkling of dried oregano, and salt and pepper. Marinate tomatoes in this mixture for at least half an hour.
2. Preheat charcoal or gas grill. Grill both sides of bread slices, then remove bread from grill and rub each slice immediately with the cut side of a garlic clove. Brush lightly with the remaining olive oil. Arrange on a large platter.

   or

   Preheat the oven to 375 degrees. Place the pieces of bread on a large baking sheet and toast them for about 10 minutes on each side. Remove and rub immediately with the cut side of a garlic clove. Brush lightly with the remaining olive oil. Arrange the toasted bread on a large platter.
3. Spread the tomato mixture on the *bruschetta* and serve immediately.

Crostini

di

Verdure

•

*Little
Toasts with
Mushroom
Vegetable
Topping*

12 servings

• This *crostini* recipe is an adaptation of the traditional chicken-liver toasts so popular in Tuscany. It is rich and delicious served as an *antipasto* or with a salad or *frittata*. The recipe amount is for one French baguette cut on the diagonal in $^1/_4$-inch slices.

4 tablespoons of extra-virgin olive oil
$^1/_2$ small onion, finely chopped
1 garlic clove, finely minced
1 small carrot, peeled and finely chopped
1 short celery stalk, finely chopped
1 tablespoon of fresh flat-leaf parsley, finely minced
$^3/4$ pound of fresh mushrooms, chopped
a pinch of crushed, dry porcini mushrooms (optional)
$^1/_4$ cup of dry white wine
$^1/_4$ cup of vegetable stock
12 slices of French bread
1 tablespoon of capers, rinsed and chopped
2 anchovy fillets, drained and chopped (optional)

1. Warm the olive oil over medium heat in a medium-sized skillet. Add the chopped onion, garlic, carrot, celery, parsley, and mushrooms and cook for 5 minutes, stirring frequently. Add wine and cook for another 3 minutes while scraping the bottom of the pan. Add the stock, lower the heat, and simmer very gently for about 10 minutes.
2. Toast the bread in a 375-degree oven for 5 minutes on each side.
3. Put the mushroom mixture into the bowl of a food processor and chop finely. Add the capers and anchovies (if desired). Stir well to blend. Spread the mixture on the toasts and serve.

OTHER TOPPINGS FOR CROSTINI:

Recipe amounts are for one French baguette cut on the diagonal in $^1/_4$-inch slices. The baguette will slice more evenly, without shredding, if partially frozen.

- 1 $^1/_3$ cups of pitted black olives (*Kalamata* or *Gaeta*)
  2 cloves of garlic
  4 tablespoons of extra-virgin olive oil (or more to taste)
  salt and freshly ground pepper to taste
  2 tablespoons of flat-leaf Italian parsley, minced

In a food processor or blender, combine the black olives and garlic with the olive oil. Pulse to purée, season with salt and pepper, and spread a layer of the mixture on each toasted crostini. Top with minced parsley.

- 2 cups of pesto (homemade, page 135 or purchased)
  8 ounces of fresh mozzarella, thinly sliced
  1 cup marinated, slivered sun-dried tomatoes (recipe follows)

Spread each crostini with one tablespoon pesto, cover with a thin slice of mozzarella, and top with a sliver of sun-dried tomato. Place on a cookie sheet and bake in a very hot oven (475 to 500 degrees) until the cheese melts (about 5 to 7 minutes; watch carefully!).

Crostini alle Olive

•

Crostini with Olives

Crostini al Pesto, Mozzarella, e Pomodori Secchi

•

Crostini with Pesto, Mozzarella, and Sun-dried Tomatoes

29

2 cups water
2 cups white vinegar
4 to 5 ounces sun-dried tomatoes
2 cups good quality olive oil (I use half extra-virgin and half olive oil)

1. Bring water and vinegar to a boil.
2. Add dried tomatoes, lower the heat and simmer for 3 to 4 minutes.
3. Drain well and rinse with cold water.
4. Put tomatoes in a large, clean bell jar and pour oil to cover. seal tightly and store on a pantry shelf. Do not refrigerate. Tomatoes will keep for months if totally covered in oil and sealed tightly. Use these succulent tomatoes for focaccia, crostini, in salads and pasta sauces.

• Although this recipe can be used as a salad, it is most often served as part of an *antipasto* buffet. Fresh mozzarella is a key ingredient, and *Mozzarella di Bufala* (imported from the area near Naples in Campania) is the ideal choice. Very ripe garden tomatoes and fresh basil are also essential.

> 8 ounces of fresh mozzarella
> 2 ripe, medium-sized tomatoes or 1 large Beefsteak tomato
> 2 tablespoons of extra-virgin olive oil
> 4 to 5 fresh basil leaves
> oregano to taste (optional)
> salt and freshly ground pepper to taste

1. Slice mozzarella 1/4-inch thick.
2. Slice tomatoes thinly with a serrated knife.
3. On a small platter, overlap slices of tomato and mozzarella.
4. Drizzle with extra-virgin olive oil and decorate with fresh basil leaves. Season with oregano (if desired), salt and pepper to taste. Serve at room temperature.

NOTE: Roasted peppers may be used in place of tomatoes when ripe, succulent tomatoes are out of season.

Insalata Caprese

•

Layered Fresh Mozzarella and Tomatoes with Basil

4 servings

Caponata

•

Sicilian Eggplant Relish

• *Caponata,* or *capunatina* in Sicilian dialect, was always part of our Sunday *antipasto* plate. When I began serving *caponata* at cocktail parties and buffet suppers, it was the one dish that always disappeared entirely. This relish is also delicious as a topping for *crostini*.

3 ripe, medium-sized eggplants (about 2 1/2 pounds)
salt (to sprinkle on eggplant)
3 tablespoons extra-virgin olive oil plus 1/3 cup pure olive oil
2 large onions, coarsely chopped
4 stalks celery, coarsely chopped
1 12-ounce can of crushed tomatoes or tomato purée
3 fresh basil leaves, slivered
1 teaspoon of salt
1/2 teaspoon of pepper
1/4 cup of capers, drained and rinsed
1 cup of small green olives, pitted and sliced
1 1/2 tablespoons of sugar, or more to taste
scant 1/4 cup of red wine vinegar

1. Remove the stems from the eggplants and discard. Cut unpeeled eggplant into 1/2-inch cubes and salt liberally; drain in a colander with a heavy weight, such as a pot or a glass mixing bowl, on top for 1 hour to allow the bitter juices to drain off. Rinse off salt, squeeze well, and dry with absorbent paper. Set aside.
2. Heat 3 tablespoons of the olive oil in a large skillet; add onions and celery, and sauté covered for 5 to 8 minutes until slightly softened. Pour in tomatoes; add basil, salt, and pepper. Simmer for 10 minutes. Add capers and olives, and cook for 5 minutes longer. Set aside.

3. In another large skillet, sauté the eggplant in $^1/_3$ cup of hot olive oil. (Add more oil if necessary to prevent sticking; eggplant absorbs a lot of oil as it cooks.) After 15 minutes, transfer the sautéed eggplant to the skillet with the onion-and-celery mixture, stirring until evenly mixed.
4. Sprinkle the mixture with sugar, pour vinegar over, and stir. Cover and simmer slowly over low heat for 10 to 15 minutes. Refrigerate for at least 24 hours, or up to three days. The flavor improves with time. Serve warm or cold as an *antipasto,* a salad, or a topping for *crostini. Caponata* may be frozen for up to three months.

Carciofi Aglio e Olio alla Menta

•

Tiny Artichokes with Extra-Virgin Olive Oil, Garlic, and Mint

4 to 5 servings as a side dish, or 8 as part of an antipasto

• Tiny fresh artichokes, available in the spring, should be used for this dish. While frozen artichoke hearts can be prepared in this way, there is no comparison in flavor with the fresh ones!

8 to 10 tiny, fresh, whole artichokes
3 tablespoons of lemon juice
1/4 cup of extra-virgin olive oil
3 to 4 cloves of garlic, finely minced
4 sprigs of fresh mint leaves, minced
salt and freshly ground pepper to taste
fresh mint leaves for garnish

1. Cut off the base and the top third of the artichokes. Remove all the tough outer leaves until only the light green, tender leaves remain. Fill a medium saucepan halfway with salted water, and add the lemon juice. Place the cleaned artichokes into the saucepan.
2. Bring the water to a boil, cover, lower the heat, and simmer for 15 to 20 minutes, or until the artichokes are very tender. Drain the artichokes, cut them in half, and set them aside.
3. Wipe out the saucepan. Put the olive oil, garlic, and mint into the saucepan, and sauté on low heat for 3 to 4 minutes. Add the artichokes and sauté on very low heat, turning gently until they are coated with the oil–mint mixture. Salt and pepper to taste. Turn off the heat after 5 minutes. The artichokes may be served immediately, or after cooling to room temperature. Garnish with fresh mint.

• Nothing is more delicious than fresh vegetables basted in extra-virgin olive oil and grilled on an open fire. A sprinkling of minced fresh herbs brings out the marvelous flavor of the vegetables.

2 medium eggplants
4 medium zucchini
$^1/_2$ cup of extra-virgin olive oil
salt and freshly ground pepper to taste
minced fresh herbs such as basil, oregano, marjoram, and parsley
balsamic vinegar (optional)

1. Preheat a charcoal or gas grill.
2. Remove both ends of the eggplant and zucchini, leaving the skin on. Cut into rounds $^1/_2$-inch to $^3/_4$-inch thick. The zucchini may be sliced vertically instead of into rounds.
3. Lay slices on cookie sheet and brush lightly with olive oil. Alternatively, the vegetables may be marinated for 15 minutes in the olive oil and herbs before grilling.
4. Grill vegetables on the grill, turning once until they are golden—approximately 4 minutes on each side. Watch carefully to prevent overcooking.
5. Immediately transfer the eggplant and zucchini slices to a platter, brush them with the remaining olive oil; sprinkle with salt and a few grindings of pepper and fresh herbs or balsamic vinegar if desired.

Melanzane e Zucchine alla Griglia

•

Grilled Eggplant and Zucchini

6 to 8 servings

Peperoni Arrostiti

•

Roasted Peppers

1 large pepper serves 2 as part of an antipasto that includes 3 or 4 other vegetables

• Roasted peppers were a constant on our *antipasto* plates at my grandparents' Sunday dinner feasts. Colorful and succulent, they complimented the sharp cheese, black olives, and other vegetables included in the antipasto. Crusty Italian bread is a must when serving roasted peppers! There are several methods of roasting peppers:

1. Preheat a charcoal or gas grill for 10 minutes. Put whole washed red, orange, yellow, or green peppers directly on the grill (any combination or all of one variety may be used). Close the lid of the grill and check in 5 to 7 minutes. Turn with long metal tongs, close the lid, and repeat the process until the peppers are evenly charred on all sides. Remove the peppers and immediately place them in brown paper bags; lunch bags are perfect, two peppers to a bag. Close the bags and leave the peppers to steam for at least 10 to 15 minutes or until cool enough to handle. Remove the stems and tops of the peppers and clean out the seeds; then peel away the strips of charred skin. Place large strips of peppers in a serving dish or plastic container for storing in the refrigerator or freezer.

2. Preheat the oven to 450 degrees. Place a pan containing a little water on the bottom rack to catch the juices from the peppers (this will prevent spills and smoking on the floor of the oven). Place the whole peppers directly on the upper oven rack, turning them every 5 to 7 minutes until evenly charred on all sides. Then proceed with the steaming and peeling steps described in the grill method of roasting peppers (#1 above).

3. If you have a gas cooktop, you can roast peppers individually. Use a long meat fork and turn each pepper over a high flame until it is charred on all sides. Then proceed with the steaming and peeling steps described in the grill method of roasting peppers (#1 above).

4. To serve roasted peppers, drizzle extra-virgin olive oil over them, and season with fresh basil, salt, and freshly ground pepper. Chopped garlic and pieces of black cured olives may also be added for flavor.

36

• This dish evokes memories of summer buffet parties my mother gave at our beach home. The presentation of the sautéed peppers and onion rings on a large round ceramic platter was stunning.

10 green frying peppers
2 cups of fine, dry bread crumbs
salt and pepper to taste
3 tablespoons of tomato purée
3 tablespoons plus 4 tablespoons of extra-virgin olive oil,
    and additional oil for sautéeing
1 tablespoon of fresh basil, minced
1 tin of flat anchovy filets, drained (optional)
1 large onion (red or white)
3 to 4 tablespoons of red wine vinegar
fresh mint leaves for garnish

1. Wash the peppers. Cut off the tops about $1/2$-inch down and set aside. Carefully seed the peppers.
2. Combine bread crumbs, salt and pepper, tomato purée, 3 tablespoons of the olive oil, and basil.
3. Fill the peppers with the bread-crumb mixture, but do not pack the filling in. Slide half of an anchovy filet (if desired) into each pepper. Replace the tops of the peppers and secure them with toothpicks.
4. In a large skillet, sauté the stuffed peppers very slowly in olive oil, turning them carefully until they are golden on all sides. Arrange the peppers in a circular pattern on a round platter.
5. Slice the onion into thin rings. Sauté the onion in 4 tablespoons of olive oil until soft. Arrange the onion rings on top of the peppers. Drizzle red wine vinegar over the peppers. Serve chilled or at room temperature, garnished with fresh mint.

Taglianelle alla Siciliana

•

Mom's Sicilian Stuffed Green Frying Peppers

10 servings

Zucchine a Scapecce

•

Fried Zucchini Slices Marinated in Extra-Virgin Olive Oil, Vinegar, and Fresh Mint

8 servings

• Think of this dish as a relish. As a child, I would include a few slices of fried zucchini in my sandwich. At the lunch table, the strong scent of vinegar provoked raised eyebrows from my table companions. I couldn't understand how everyone didn't love this tasty dish!

4 medium zucchini
$1/2$ cup of extra-virgin olive oil, or more as needed
1 onion, sliced thin
$1/4$ cup of red wine vinegar
fresh mint leaves for garnish

1. Wash zucchini well and cut off both ends. Slice on the diagonal about $1/4$-inch thick.
2. Heat $1/4$ cup of the olive oil and sauté one layer of zucchini slices in it until golden. Repeat the process with the remaining oil until all of the zucchini is sautéed. Transfer the zucchini to a glass or ceramic serving platter and arrange the slices in an overlapping pattern.
3. Sauté the onion rings just until translucent, adding oil if more is needed. Arrange the onion rings on top of the fried zucchini. Pour the vinegar into the skillet and allow it to simmer for 2 to 3 minutes. Pour the vinegar over the zucchini and onions. Garnish with mint leaves and chill. This dish may be served cold or at room temperature.

• I remember Mom serving these marinated mushrooms at buffet parties. They are delicate yet spicy, and they complement just about anything they are served with.

2 cups of white vinegar
4 pounds of whole medium-sized mushroom caps, wiped clean
3 cloves of garlic
juice of one lemon
$^1/_3$ cup of extra-virgin olive oil
2 teaspoons of crushed red pepper flakes (optional)
1 teaspoon of oregano
salt and freshly ground pepper to taste
6 fresh basil leaves, slivered

1. Bring 4 cups of water and the vinegar to a boil in a large Dutch oven. Add the mushrooms, bring back to a boil, and turn off the heat. Cover the pot and let it stand for 15 minutes.
2. Drain the mushrooms and rinse with cold water.
3. Place mushrooms in a glass or ceramic serving bowl and mix with all of the remaining ingredients.
4. Refrigerate for several hours or overnight. Serve cold or at room temperature. Remove the garlic cloves before serving.

Funghi Sott' Olio di Mamma

•

Mom's Marinated Mushrooms

Serves 16–20 as an antipasto dish

Insalata di Olive in Marinata

•

Aunt Edith's Sicilian Olive Salad

Serves 10 as an antipasto dish

• No *antipasti* buffet would be complete without dishes of succulent olives. Good-quality black olives such as *Gaeta* are delicious served by themselves, while large Sicilian green olives may be pitted, breaded, and fried, or cracked, pitted, and marinated as in my aunt's very tasty salad.

1 pound of large Sicilian green olives, cracked and pitted
2 stalks of celery from the heart, with leaves, chopped in small pieces
2 tablespoons of capers, drained and rinsed
crushed red pepper to taste
1 teaspoon of oregano
$^1/_4$ cup of extra-virgin olive oil
3 tablespoons of red wine vinegar

1. Put the olives, celery, capers, red pepper, and oregano in a glass or ceramic bowl.
2. Add the olive oil and vinegar.
3. Toss and chill for several hours or overnight.
4. Serve cold or at room temperature.

Insalate

Chef Angelo Chiavaroli at Market, Abruzzo

RECIPES

- *Panzanella*
  ITALIAN BREAD AND TOMATO SALAD

- *Insalata di Farro per L'Estate di Rolando Beramendi*
  ROLANDO BERAMENDI'S SUMMER FARRO SALAD
  WITH TOMATOES AND CANNELLINI BEANS

- *Insalata di Indivia e Radicchio*
  ENDIVE AND RADICCHIO SALAD WITH BALSAMIC DRESSING

- *Carciofi al Tegame*
  STEWED ARTICHOKES WITH TARRAGON-DILL VINAIGRETTE

- *Insalata Mista*
  MIXED GREEN SALAD WITH OIL AND VINEGAR DRESSING

- *Insalata di Finocchio con Arancia*
  FENNEL AND ORANGE SALAD

- *Insalata di Rucola e Pomodori con Funghi Porcini alla Griglia*
  ARUGULA AND TOMATO SALAD WITH GRILLED PORCINI
  MUSHROOMS

- *Insalata di Pomodori*
  GARDEN-FRESH TOMATO SALAD

*A*T OUR FESTIVE Sunday family dinners at my grandparents' home, salad always arrived at the end of the meal. This was also the way I was served in the restaurants of Italy when I studied Italian at the University of Florence. Today, though, there is more flexibility with salad, even in Italy. Salad may be an *antipasto,* or it may be served at the end of the meal to cleanse the palate before dessert, such as *Insalata Mista,* (page 50). In our Sicilian family, we did not eat cold pasta in any form. My mother shuddered at the mere idea of it. But we did enjoy many variations of the simple *insalata mista,* such as *Panzanella* (page 45). This salad is made from the *mollica,* or insides, of coarse-textured Italian bread combined with very ripe tomatoes and extra-virgin olive oil. *Panzanella* is even better when made ahead, so it is a perfect dish to take on picnics or to serve as part of a buffet. A variation of this salad, found in this chapter, is my friend Rolando Beramendi's Summer Farro Salad (page 46). Farro is a cereal grain similar to spelt that swells when soaked in water, but farro has more body and retains its bite and texture even if it's reheated. The farro takes the place of the bread in the traditional *Panzanella* recipe and gives the dish a marvelous texture.

I enjoy all salads, but one of my favorites is a simple salad of freshly picked summer tomatoes, sweet red onion, fresh basil, and extra-virgin olive oil, especially when it is served with a vegetable *frittata.* My children's favorite substitute for a green salad is steamed whole artichokes served with a vinaigrette into which you dip the tender leaves and heart.

When I was a child, *finocchio* (fennel) was always included in our family's holiday dinner menu. This delicious, crispy, licorice-flavored white bulb, with the long fuzzy leaves resembling fresh dill, is sold by greengrocers in America as "anise." Nowadays, after the main course in our traditional Thanksgiving and Christmas dinners, my sisters and I serve the fennel raw, cut into wedges, with heaping bowls of roasted almonds, walnuts, hazelnuts, chestnuts, and fresh fruits. Fennel is a welcome addition to any meal; it is very refreshing, and is considered by the Italians to be a digestive. In this chapter, you will find a recipe for a special salad of blood oranges and fennel that I hope you will try (see *Insalata di Finocchio con Arancia*, p. 51).

The most important ingredient in preparing these salad recipes is the high-quality extra-virgin olive oil. It is expensive, but usually you need very little to bring out the flavors of the raw salad greens, artichokes, mushrooms, and vine-ripened tomatoes. Always pick produce of top quality and freshness, and even the simplest salad will become a special creation.

Finally, if you have a patch of land near your home, big or small, or a terrace that can accommodate large clay pots, I urge you to consider growing your own salad greens and herbs next summer. There is no equal to homegrown lettuce, spinach, arugula, tomatoes, cucumbers, parsley, basil, and mint. The little time and effort you invest in the early spring will yield rewards throughout the summer and into the fall.

• *Panzanella* is a salad that makes excellent use of stale bread and a bumper crop of vine-ripened tomatoes. It is perfect to take on picnics in the country or at the beach, as it holds together beautifully and tastes better if made ahead.

 *Panzanella*

•

*Italian Bread
and Tomato
Salad*

*6 to 8
servings*

1 to 2 cups of stale, coarse bread, decrusted and soaked in water
3 to 4 large ripe tomatoes, cut into chunks
1 clove of garlic, minced
1/2 cup of fresh basil leaves, torn
1 medium red onion, minced
1/2 cup of extra-virgin olive oil
4 tablespoons of wine vinegar
salt and freshly ground pepper to taste

1. Squeeze the water out of the bread, and crumble it into small pieces in a salad bowl.
2. Add the tomato chunks, garlic, basil, and onion.
3. Whisk together the olive oil, vinegar, salt, and pepper in a small bowl. Pour over the bread mixture and toss. Let the salad sit for about half an hour at room temperature before serving to allow the flavors to blend.

Insalata di Farro per L'Estate di Rolando Beramendi

•

Rolando Beramendi's Summer Farro Salad with Tomatoes and Cannellini Beans

6 to 8 servings

• Rolando Beramendi, the founder of the Avignonesi Wine and Food Workshop in Tuscany, introduced me to this delicious salad when he taught a summer class at my cooking school, *Cucina Casalinga*. The farro grain is a wonderful substitute for the stale bread in the traditional *Panzanella* salad. This salad transports beautifully for picnics and parties.

1 pound of farro
$^1/_2$ cup of extra-virgin olive oil
2 garlic cloves, peeled and left whole
6 vine-ripened tomatoes, halved and cut into slices
1 cucumber, scraped and cut into wedges
1 red onion, cut into small pieces
1 15 $^1/_2$-ounce can of *cannellini* beans
a handful of fresh basil leaves
salt and freshly ground pepper to taste

1. Put the farro in a bowl and cover with cold water. Let it sit for 2 hours. Drain and discard the water.
2. In a large stock pot, cover the farro with fresh cold water and bring to a boil. Cook for about 40 minutes until *al dente*. For this particular recipe, the texture of the farro should be very soft, a bit more tender than *al dente*. Drain and rinse with cold water, transfer to a large ceramic glass bowl, and immediately drizzle $^1/_4$ cup of the olive oil on the farro. Let it cool.
3. In a sauté pan, heat the rest of the olive oil and the garlic over very low flame for about a minute. Once you turn the flame off, discard the garlic.
4. Add the tomatoes, cucumber, onion, and beans to the farro. Drizzle the garlic-flavored olive oil over the farro mixture. Cut the basil into fine ribbons, add it to the mixture, and toss together with salt and pepper.

TIP   This salad actually tastes better the day after it's made.

• This salad is very elegant because of the use of special ingredients: Belgian endive and radicchio. The extra-virgin olive oil and balsamic vinegar dressing further enhances this dish.

4 large Belgian endives, cut crosswise *or* 2 hearts of romaine
    lettuce, torn into pieces
1 large or 2 medium heads of radicchio, torn into bite-sized pieces

VINAIGRETTE DRESSING:

3/4 cup of extra-virgin olive oil
3 tablespoons of balsamic vinegar
salt and freshly ground pepper to taste

1. In a large serving bowl, toss the endive slices and radicchio pieces.
2. In a small bowl, whisk together the olive oil and vinegar.
3. Pour the vinaigrette over the salad and toss to coat.
4. Season with salt and pepper to taste and toss once more.

Insalata di Indivia e Radicchio

•

Endive and Radicchio Salad with Balsamic Dressing

6 to 8 servings

Carciofi

al

Tegame

•

Stewed
Artichokes
with
Tarragon-Dill
Vinaigrette

6 servings

• My children, at an early age, began eating artichokes cooked this way. Of course, if each did not have a whole artichoke there was always the question of who would get the sweet, tender heart!

6 whole artichokes
6 thin lemon slices
Tarragon-Dill Vinaigrette *or* Extra-Virgin Olive Oil with
    Lemon Juice *or* Balsamic Vinegar Dressing

1. Cut the stems off the artichokes so that they can stand upright. Cut off the top third of each artichoke and use scissors to trim off the pointed tips of all the leaves.
2. Place each artichoke on top of a lemon slice and tie them together securely with string.
3. Stand the artichokes in a stainless steel or enamel Dutch oven so that they fit snugly. Fill the pot with lightly salted water to halfway up the artichokes. Cover and boil gently until tender, about 30 to 40 minutes. Test by piercing the center of the artichoke with a fork. It should be soft. Add more boiling water as necessary.
4. Remove the artichokes, untie the strings, remove the lemon slices, and place the artichokes on individual dishes. Serve each artichoke with a small bowl of dressing for dipping.

- $^1/_8$ cup of tarragon vinegar
  1 heaping teaspoon of Dijon mustard
  1 clove of garlic, crushed
  3 tablespoons of fresh or dried dill
  $^1/_2$ teaspoon of salt
  freshly ground pepper to taste
  1 cup of oil ($^1/_2$ olive oil and $^1/_2$ extra-virgin olive oil)

Put all ingredients in a covered jar and shake until well blended.

ALTERNATE METHOD:

Put all the ingredients except the oil in the bowl of a food processor. Turn processor on and pour in the oil in a stream while processing. The dressing will become creamy in seconds.

ALTERNATE DRESSING:

- 1 cup of extra-virgin olive oil
  juice of one lemon or 3 tablespoons of balsamic vinegar
  salt and freshly ground pepper

Whisk all ingredients together in a small bowl.

Tarragon-Dill Vinaigrette

•

1 cup

Extra-Virgin Olive Oil with Lemon Juice or Balsamic Vinegar Dressing

•

1 cup

49

Insalata Mista

Mixed Green Salad with Oil and Vinegar Dressing

8 servings

• Italians most often serve a simple salad of mixed greens, tomato, and cucumber, with a dressing of good-quality extra-virgin olive oil and vinegar. In the south of Italy—Naples, Amalfi, and Sicily—you would more likely be served this salad with the juice of their luscious fresh lemons in place of the vinegar.

1 head of romaine lettuce, broken into bite-sized pieces
2 cups of mixed greens (chicory, arugula, romaine, etc.)
1 cucumber, skinned and sliced into thin discs
2 ripe medium tomatoes, cut into wedges
1/2 cup of extra-virgin olive oil
2 tablespoons of red wine vinegar *or* the juice of one medium fresh lemon
salt and freshly ground pepper to taste

1. Place the romaine, mixed greens, cucumber slices, and tomato wedges in a large salad bowl.
2. Pour extra-virgin olive oil over the greens. Sprinkle with vinegar or lemon juice, salt, and a few grindings of pepper. Toss well and serve on individual salad plates.

• Blood oranges are available in Sicily at the end of winter. Juice from these sweet oranges is often served as part of the *prima colazione* (breakfast). Fine greengrocers here in the United States also import these oranges, but navel oranges can be substituted for the blood oranges if you cannot find them.

2 small fennel bulbs or 1 large
3 oranges (blood or naval)
1 medium red onion, sliced thin (optional)
$^1/_4$ cup of extra-virgin olive oil
balsamic vinegar or freshly squeezed lemon juice (optional)
salt and freshly ground pepper to taste

1. Wash the fennel and remove the outer leaves if dark. Cut each bulb length-wise into quarters and then slice as thinly as possible.
2. Peel oranges, being careful to remove all of the white pith. Slice oranges into thin rounds.
3. Arrange slices of orange on individual plates. Top with fennel slices and then onion if desired.
4. Drizzle extra-virgin olive oil over each plate and add a sprinkling of balsamic vinegar or lemon juice if desired.
5. Season with salt and pepper to taste.

Insalata di Finocchio con Arancia

•

Fennel and Orange Salad

6 to 8 servings

Insalata di Rucola e Pomodori con Funghi Porcini alla Griglia

•

Arugula and Tomato Salad with Grilled Porcini Mushrooms

8 servings

• This salad may easily be served as an *antipasto* course since large mushrooms such as the fresh porcini or portabella variety are very rich. The balsamic vinegar complements the woodsy flavor of the grilled mushrooms. A good-quality extra-virgin olive oil is the key to bringing out all of the flavors in this salad.

1 cup of extra-virgin olive oil
1 clove of garlic, minced
2 large, fresh porcini or portabella mushrooms
2 large bunches of arugula, well-washed with stems removed
4 ripe medium tomatoes, cut into wedges
1/4 cup of balsamic vinegar (or more, to taste)
 salt and freshly ground pepper to taste

1. Wipe the mushrooms with a damp cloth, scrape the stems, and slice the mushrooms thickly. Mix half of the olive oil with all of the minced garlic, and marinate the mushroom slices in this mixture for 15 minutes.
2. Preheat a charcoal or gas grill, and grill the mushrooms until tender and brown (about 5 minutes).
3. Arrange the arugula and tomato wedges on individual serving plates and top each with 2 or 3 slices of the mushrooms.
4. Drizzle the remaining olive oil and the balsamic vinegar over each serving, and season with salt and pepper.

• This salad is best made in the late summer with fresh tomatoes picked right out of the garden. It was my father's favorite salad with the addition of the red onion. It is milder if the onion is omitted. With either version, fresh crusty Italian bread for dipping in the flavorful juices of the tomatoes and the olive oil is a must!

4 medium vine-ripened tomatoes, cut into wedges
1 small red onion, slivered (optional)
4 fresh basil leaves, shredded
1/2 teaspoon of dried oregano
salt and freshly ground pepper to taste
1/3 cup of extra-virgin olive oil
3 tablespoons of ice cold water

1. Place the tomato wedges in a glass or ceramic bowl.
2. Add onion slivers (if desired), basil, oregano, and salt and pepper to taste.
3. Pour the olive oil over the tomatoes and herbs, and toss.
4. Add ice water and toss again. Serve immediately in small, deep bowls.

•

*Garden-Fresh
Tomato Salad*

*4 to 6
servings as
a side salad*

Primi Piatti: Zuppe e Minestre

Chef Carlo Cioni, "Ristorante Da Delfina," Tuscany

RECIPES

- *Brodo di Verdura*
  VEGETABLE BROTH

- *Pastina in Brodo*
  TINY PASTA IN BROTH

- *Zuppa di Scarola e Fagioli*
  ESCAROLE AND BEAN SOUP

- *Minestrone al Pesto*
  HEARTY VEGETABLE SOUP WITH PESTO

- *Zuppa di Bietole e Pomodoro con Linguine*
  SWISS CHARD AND TOMATO SOUP WITH LINGUINE

- *Stracciatella di Spinaci e Uova al Parmigiano*
  SPINACH SOUP WITH EGG AND PARMESAN CHEESE

- *Minestra di Porri, Zucchine e Zucchine Gialle*
  LEEK, ZUCCHINI, AND YELLOW SQUASH SOUP

- *Zuppa di Mamma*
  MOM'S ITALIAN "MATZO" BALL SOUP

- *Zuppa di Lenticchie*
  LENTIL SOUP

- *Minestra di Fagiolini, Pomodori e Patate di Nonna Peppina*
  GRANDMA PEPPINA'S STRING BEAN, TOMATO, AND POTATO SOUP

- *Riso e Verza*
  RICE AND CABBAGE SOUP

- *La Minestra di Pane Ribollita di Chef Piero Ferrini*
  CHEF PIERO FERRINI'S TUSCAN BREAD AND VEGETABLE SOUP

- *Zuppa di Pasta e Fagioli alla Toscana*
  TUSCAN PASTA AND BEAN SOUP

- *Conchigliette con Ceci e Pomodoro*
  TINY SHELL PASTA WITH TOMATO AND CHICK PEA SOUP

*I*N THE UNIVERSAL LANGUAGE of food, all agree that soup means comfort. This could not be better illustrated in Italian cuisine than by the warm and wonderful story written by Tomie dePaola, "Watch Out for the Chicken Feet in Your Soup." In the story, Joey brings his friend, Eugene, home to meet his Italian Grandma, who serves them heaping bowls of her homemade chicken soup as well as spaghetti and homemade bread. The love in Grandma's kitchen envelopes the boys and leaves the reader nostalgic for childhood days and the comfort of steaming soup in a warm kitchen with Grandma. My sisters and I were fortunate to have such memories in Grandma Peppina's kitchen, dunking our crusty Italian bread in her luscious String Bean, Tomato, and Potato Soup (page 71).

Many American children today subsist largely on fast food and frozen pizzas, yet I am happy to say that, in my cooking school, the "Kids Cook Italian" series always fills up. And it is the soup class—particularly the part about minestrone—that's always in demand. Mothers often say that their children do not eat vegetables, but I find that children who take an active part in preparing their meals are more likely to eat the results.

Once I had eleven children in my soup class. In the minestrone recipe I taught them, there are eight or nine fresh vegetables in addition to the beans and rice. The students happily diced and chopped, and in the end almost all asked for second helpings.

Many Italian soup recipes resulted from the need to use leftovers. In Italy, nothing is tossed out if it can help create something nourishing and delicious. For example, a soup like *ribollita* (Tuscan Bread and Vegetable Soup, page 74) has long been in the Italian soup repertoire. Dishes that were once part of the *cucina povera* (poor people's cooking) now are enjoyed in both modest and noble Italian homes. Simple but hearty vegetable soups are often served daily as *primi piatti* (first courses) in place of pasta or *risotto*. In America, these filling and nutritious soups—especially those including beans, lentils, grains, rice, or pasta—

are often used as main courses, served with a salad and a crusty loaf of bread or an herbed *focaccia*.

All of the soups in this chapter use the recipe for *Brodo di Verdura* (Vegetable Broth, page 61). Making homemade vegetable broth is easy and rewarding. The vegetables are coarsely chopped and added to boiling water. A little extra-virgin olive oil is added for flavor. For a more intense flavor, the vegetables can be sautéed or roasted for 10 minutes in the olive oil before the water is added, but I prefer to follow the former method, which results in a lighter stock.

The vegetables used to make the broth should be fresh and well cleaned. In addition to regular yellow onions, I add leeks, which bring a very sweet flavor to any soup or sauce. For a delicate soup recipe such as *Minestra di Porri, Zucchine e Zucchine Gialle* (Leek, Zucchini, and Yellow Squash Soup, page 68), I use leeks in place of yellow onions. Just be forewarned that leeks hold dirt and grit, and should be sliced lengthwise and then washed between each fold. Most recipes use only the white root end and the light green part above it. The dark leafy portion of the leek should be cut off and discarded.

I try to make my vegetable broth several hours before using it in other recipes; that gives the flavors of the vegetables a chance to blend and deepen. I often make my vegetable broth first thing in the morning so that by dinnertime, when the broth is reheated, it tastes as if it had been made the day before. Unlike meat stocks, vegetable broths have little fat to skim off the top after the broth has been refrigerated. Strain the broth before separating it into containers, making sure that you press the vegetable solids against the strainer to extract all the flavorful juices. Individual cubes of broth made by freezing the liquid in ice trays can be used later to flavor soups and sauces.

Many of the recipes in this chapter contain beans. I have listed canned beans in the ingredients because they can be readily available if kept on the pantry shelf. Since our lifestyles in America are so hectic, I think we are more apt to make these nutritious soups if we don't have to worry about remembering to soak the beans overnight (or a minimum of four hours) before we use them. But if you want to use dried beans, there are shortcuts. Dried beans can be speed-soaked in a pressure cooker (following the manufacturer's directions), or, to speed up the softening process they can be boiled for two minutes, removed from the heat, and then left to soak for one hour. Drain and proceed to cook them according to the recipe.

Pasta added to vegetable soups should always be partially pre-cooked, but undercooked, because it will finish cooking in the soup broth. Cook the pasta in salted water, then drain it, to prevent the release of excess starch into the soup which would make it too thick. The pasta should be added at the last minute, according to the recipe, to avoid absorbing all the broth. When reheating a rich soup that contains pasta or rice, you may have to add more water or broth.

Many of the recipes in this chapter were traditionally made with a base that included animal fat for flavoring, most often, *pancetta* (a kind of bacon). To insure the tastiest soup possible, I use extra-virgin olive oil to sauté the onion, garlic, celery, and carrots, which form the basis for these classic soups. The rich, fruity flavor of the extra-virgin olive oil really shines through. This healthy substitute for pork flavoring justifies the added expense of the fine-quality olive oil.

In this age of frozen, canned, and packaged foods, there is still no substitute for the real thing. Treat yourself and your family to the joy of homemade soups. The smiles and compliments to the cook will be effusive. A final benefit: all of these soups freeze well and can be defrosted at a moment's notice to provide a nourishing meal at the end of a busy day.

• Vegetable broth is easy to make and is used not only as stock for other soups, but in making vegetable *risotto* dishes as well. Many different pasta shapes may be added to this rich broth, such as *capelli d'angelo* (angel hair), *orzo* (rice-shaped pasta), or any variety of *tortellini* or *cappelletti* (filled, hat-shaped pasta).

1 large onion, coarsely chopped
2 medium leeks, split lengthwise and then cut into
    1/4-inch slices (white and light green parts only)
2 to 3 garlic cloves, smashed
2 stalks of celery with leaves, diced
2 large carrots, peeled and diced
10 to 12 peppercorns
2 large sprigs of fresh Italian flat-leaf parsley
3 to 4 fresh basil leaves
2 large bay leaves
2 fresh plum tomatoes, quartered, or 1/4 cup of crushed
    canned tomatoes
2 tablespoons extra-virgin olive oil
salt to taste

1. Bring 12 cups of water to a boil. Add onion, leeks, garlic, celery, carrots, peppercorns, and herbs, and return to boiling.
2. Add tomatoes and extra-virgin olive oil, lower heat, and simmer broth partially covered for about 1 1/2 hours. Add salt to taste. Turn off heat, cover pot, and allow to stand until completely cool. Strain the vegetables, pressing the solids against the strainer to extract all of the vegetable juices, and pour the broth into containers to refrigerate or freeze for later use.

Pastina in Brodo

Tiny Pasta in Broth

2 servings

• One of the few pasta shapes that can be boiled directly in water or broth, *pastina* is the perfect dish for children who like a warm, filling snack after school. My youngest son, Tony, often prepares a heaping bowl of *pastina* as soon as he arrives from school. If homemade broth is not available, bouillon cubes or packets can be added to the water for a quick broth.

3 cups of homemade Vegetable Broth (page 61) *or*
      3 cups of water and 3 packets or cubes of bouillon
6 ounces of *pastina* ($^1/_2$ box)
2 tablespoon of butter (optional)
3 tablespoons of Parmesan cheese

1. Bring the broth to a boil and or boil the water and add bouillon packets or cubes, then add pastina. Stir well and lower heat. Let pasta cook until it has swelled and thickened (about 4 to 6 minutes).
2. Pour into bowls and add butter, if desired, and a sprinkling of Parmesan cheese.

• This hearty soup is even better when made several hours ahead, or even the day before, and reheated. Crisp, seeded Italian bread sticks are delicious served alongside.

1 head of escarole
1 medium onion, coarsely chopped
2 stalks of celery, coarsely chopped
3 cloves of garlic, finely minced
3 to 4 tablespoons of extra-virgin olive oil
1 15 1/2-ounce can of *cannellini* beans, drained
4 ounces of tomato sauce
2 cups of Vegetable Broth (page 61) and 2 cups escarole water
salt and freshly ground pepper to taste

1. Wash escarole leaves thoroughly and boil in 5 quarts of salted water until limp (about 5 minutes). Drain and reserve the water.
2. In a large stockpot, sauté the chopped onion, celery, and garlic in olive oil until soft. Add escarole and sauté for 5 minutes more.
3. Add *cannellini* beans and tomato sauce. Mix well.
4. Add the broth and 2 cups (or more, to taste) of the escarole water to the vegetable mixture until it is soupy. Salt and pepper to taste.
5. Simmer, partially covered, over a low flame for 15 to 20 minutes.

VARIATION   1 cup of small macaroni (such as *ditali*), precooked and drained, may be added right before serving.

63

Minestrone al Pesto

•

Hearty Vegetable Soup with Pesto

8 to 10 servings

• My mother gave me this tip years ago: When fresh vegetables are not in season, save one cup of frozen vegetables and beans each time you prepare them for your family's dinner. After gathering a variety of five or six different vegetables, you are ready to make a minestrone from the freezer. Adding fresh leeks and escarole or cabbage will guarantee a fresh, yummy soup even out of season.

3 tablespoons of olive oil (preferably extra-virgin)
1 cup of chopped onion or 1 large cleaned leek, sliced lengthwise
     and finely diced (use the white and light green parts only)
2 cloves of garlic, finely minced
2 medium carrots, diced
1 cup of green beans, cut into 1-inch lengths
2 medium zucchini (unpeeled), cut into $1/2$-inch cubes
2 to 3 small potatoes, peeled and diced into $1/2$-inch cubes
$1/2$ pound of fresh asparagus, scraped and cut into 1-inch lengths
6 cups of Vegetable Broth (page 61)
1 small head of escarole, torn and blanched for 2 to 3 minutes and drained
     (reserve 2 cups of liquid) or 1 small head of cabbage, shredded
1 cup of *cannellini, ceci* (canned), or red kidney beans
2 plum tomatoes, peeled, seeded, and chopped, or 3 tablespoons
     of crushed tomatoes
1 cup of small peas
2 tablespoons of parsley, minced
3 basil leaves, torn
1 sprig of rosemary

salt and freshly ground pepper to taste

1 small piece of Parmesan rind (optional)

1 1/2 cups of small pasta, such as *tubettini,* undercooked
and drained, or 1/2 cup of *arborio* rice (uncooked)

1 tablespoon of *pesto* (page 92) per serving (optional)

grated Parmesan cheese

1. In a heavy Dutch oven, heat the olive oil, chopped onion or leek, and garlic, and sauté until soft but not brown.
2. Add the carrots, green beans, zucchini, potatoes, and asparagus, and sauté for 10 minutes.
3. Add the broth, reserved vegetable cooking water, escarole or cabbage, beans, tomatoes, peas, seasonings and herbs, and Parmesan rind (if desired), and simmer for 1 hour until vegetables are tender.
4. Add cooked pasta or raw rice and cook an additional 10 to 15 minutes. Top each serving with a dollop of pesto, and serve with grated Parmesan cheese.

• Swiss chard grows in our garden from June until the hard frost in late fall. My husband and I met when we were 16 years old. The first time I invited him for dinner was on the spur of the moment and my mother was preparing Swiss chard and tomato soup with linguine—a Sicilian dish we all loved. She was sure, however, that this boy from Minnesota would not find it to his liking. What a surprise—he asked for seconds!

1 1/2 pounds of Swiss chard
3 cloves of garlic
3 tablespoons of olive oil (preferably extra-virgin)
1 14-ounce can crushed tomatoes
3 to 4 large basil leaves, torn into pieces
salt and freshly ground pepper to taste
1/2 pound of *linguine*, cut into 2-inch lengths
freshly grated Parmesan or romano cheese (optional)

1. Discard all discolored stems and leaves of the Swiss chard. Wash it well, rinsing several times, and cut the stems into 3-inch lengths. Cut the leaves into 3- to 4-inch lengths.
2. Fill a 6-quart soup pot halfway with salted water, and bring the water to a boil. Add the chard leaves and stems, and boil until tender (about 8 minutes). Drain, reserving the chard and 2 cups of the liquid. Wipe out the pot.
3. In the same pot, sauté the garlic in the olive oil until translucent. Add the crushed tomatoes, basil, salt, and pepper to taste. Simmer for 10 minutes. Add the drained Swiss chard, and the reserved liquid.
4. Bring 4 quarts of salted water to a boil, add the broken linguine pieces and cook until *al dente* (5 minutes). Drain the pasta and add it to the Swiss chard-tomato mixture.
5. Simmer soup on low heat for 5 minutes more. Serve immediately. Pass grated cheese separately.

• This is our children's favorite soup. I began serving it to them as small babies. The egg and Parmesan cheese sweeten the usually bitter flavor of the spinach.

1 pound of fresh leaf spinach
3 cloves of garlic
3 tablespoons of olive oil (preferably extra-virgin)
1 cup water
salt
1 egg plus 3 tablespoons water
3 tablespoons of freshly grated Parmesan cheese
freshly ground pepper

1. Break off the tough spinach stems. Rinse the leaves well and drain in a colander.
2. In a large pot, sauté the garlic in the olive oil until translucent, being careful not to burn the garlic.
3. Add the wet spinach, 1 cup of water, and salt to taste. Cover and cook until the spinach is wilted (about 5 minutes).
4. Lightly beat the egg with the water and Parmesan cheese.
5. Add the egg-cheese mixture to the simmering spinach, swirling the mixture with a fork. Add freshly ground pepper and serve with crusty bread or bread sticks.

Stracciatella di Spinaci e Uova alla Parmigiana

•

Spinach Soup with Egg and Parmesan Cheese

3 servings

Minestra di Porri, Zucchine e Zucchine Gialle

•

Leek, Zucchini, and Yellow Squash Soup

5 to 6 servings

• Leeks are sweeter and more delicate than yellow onions, and they make this soup especially light and flavorful.

2 to 3 cloves of garlic, finely minced
2 medium leeks, rinsed well and chopped (use white and light
  green parts only)
4 to 5 tablespoons of extra-virgin olive oil
1 1/2 pounds of zucchini (about 4 medium) and 1 1/2 pounds of
  yellow squash, (about 3 medium), ends removed, diced
3 cups of Vegetable Broth (page 61)
1 medium potato, peeled and diced
salt and freshly ground pepper to taste
1 tablespoon of fresh, Italian flat-leaf parsley, minced
3 fresh basil leaves, shredded
Parmesan cheese (optional)

1. In a large soup pot, sauté the leeks and garlic in the olive oil until transparent.
2. Add the zucchini and yellow squash and cook, covered, until they are softened but not limp.
3. Add the vegetable broth, potato, salt, pepper, and herbs, and simmer for 15 to 20 minutes.
4. Sprinkle each serving with Parmesan cheese if desired.

VARIATIONS   Tiny macaroni (1 cup of cooked pasta shells or *tubetti*) may be added to the soup before serving, or add 1/2 cup of *arborio* rice 15 minutes before the soup is finished. A sprinkling of Parmesan cheese adds the final flavorful touch.

• Even though she was Sicilian, my mother made great Jewish Matzo ball soup. For a quick Italian version, however, she used the insides of crusty bread to make these delicious dumplings.

2 eggs
2 tablespoons of Italian flat-leaf parsley, chopped
3 tablespoons of grated Parmesan cheese
salt and freshly ground pepper
a dash of nutmeg
4 to 5 slices of Italian bread
4 cups of Vegetable Broth (page 61)

1. In a medium bowl, lightly beat the eggs. Blend in the parsley, Parmesan cheese, salt, pepper, and a dash of nutmeg.
2. Remove the crusts from the bread, and process it in a food processor until coarse pieces are formed; do not make the crumbs too fine. Add the bread crumbs to the egg mixture and stir until sticky.
3. Wet your hands and make balls the size of small walnuts. Put them on a plate, cover, and refrigerate them for 1 hour.
4. Bring the broth to a rolling boil. Drop the dumplings gently into the broth. Lower the heat, cover the pot, and cook until "matzo" balls puff up. Uncover and continue to cook for 2 to 3 minutes.

Zuppa di Mamma

•

Mom's Italian "Matzo" Ball Soup

4 servings

Zuppa di Lenticchie

•

Lentil Soup

6 servings

• Chef Alfonso Mazzacano shared this recipe with us at the School of Traditional Neopolitan Cuisine at the Hotel Sirenuse in Positano. The simplicity of preparation and the fabulous taste make this soup a real winner and a favorite of mine.

18 ounces of dried green or brown lentils
2 bouillon cubes
4 medium tomatoes, peeled and finely chopped
2 small leeks, well cleaned and dried (the white part only),
    chopped into $1/4$-inch pieces
2 cloves of garlic, finely chopped
4 tablespoons of chopped, fresh Italian flat-leaf parsley
6 tablespoons of extra-virgin olive oil
salt and freshly ground pepper to taste
whole wheat croutons for garnish or $1/2$ pound of small cooked
    pasta, such as *ditalini* (little thimbles) (optional)

1. Carefully check the lentils for any stones or other particles. Place lentils in a bowl, cover them with cold water, and soak for 1 to 2 hours. Drain, rinse well under cold running water, and drain again.
2. Place the lentils in a large saucepan with 6 cups of cold water and the bouillon cubes. Add the tomatoes, leeks, garlic, and parsley. Stir in the olive oil and season with salt and pepper.
3. Bring the mixture to a boil, then lower it to a simmer and cook the lentils for 1 to 1 $1/2$ hours or until they are tender. If the soup dries out too much, add a little more boiling water. Serve with croutons or pasta.

TIP   Add a little extra-virgin olive oil at the end for flavor. If you use pasta, boil it separately and drain it before adding it to the lentils.

• Grandma Peppina often served this soup to us for lunch with crusty Italian bread for dipping.

1 1/2 pounds of whole string beans, stem ends removed, cut into thirds
3 whole cloves of garlic
3 tablespoons of extra-virgin olive oil
1 28-ounce can of crushed tomatoes
2 medium potatoes, peeled and cut into 3/4-inch cubes
2 tablespoons of fresh basil leaves, shredded
1/2 cup of water
salt and freshly ground pepper to taste

1. Bring 2 cups salted water to a boil in a saucepan. Add beans and cook just until crisp tender, about 6 minutes. Drain and set aside.
2. In the same saucepan, sauté the garlic cloves in the olive oil until transparent, not brown.
3. Add the tomatoes, potatoes, basil, 1/2 cup of water, and salt and pepper to taste. Simmer partially covered 20 minutes or until the potatoes are tender, adding more water if necessary. Add the beans and cook for an additional 5 minutes.
4. Serve in soup bowls with crusty Italian bread.

Minestra di Fagiolini, Pomodoro e Patate di Nonna Peppina

•

Grandma Peppina's String Bean, Tomato, and Potato Soup

5 to 6 servings

Riso e Verza

•

Rice and Cabbage Soup

6 to 8 servings

• Almost a *risotto* rather than a soup, this dish is very satisfying as a main course. Even non-cabbage-lovers will enjoy the flavors of this wonderful soup from Antonio Sersale, director of the cooking program at the Sirenuse Hotel in Positano.

FOR THE BROTH:

2 onions, peeled and quartered
1 carrot, peeled and cut into pieces
1 celery stalk, cut into pieces
a few sprigs of Italian flat-leaf parsley
1 bay leaf
2 cups of vegetable bouillon
salt to taste

FOR THE CABBAGE:

$^1/_2$ onion, finely chopped
1 small celery stalk, finely chopped
4 tablespoons of extra-virgin olive oil
1 $^1/_2$ pounds of cabbage (Savoy, if available), chopped
salt and freshly ground pepper to taste
2 cups of *arborio* rice
1 cup of freshly grated Parmesan cheese
1 cup of hard or semi-soft cheese (*Bel paese, scamorza,* or mozzarella), diced
2 tablespoons of grated provolone cheese (optional)

1. Make the broth by placing the vegetables and herbs in a saucepan with 5 cups of water and the vegetable bouillon. Bring to a boil and simmer for 30 minutes. Strain. Season with salt.
2. In a large stockpot, stir the onion and celery into the olive oil. Cover over low-to-medium heat until the onion is translucent and golden. Stir in the cabbage and then add the broth mixture. Season with salt and pepper. Cook over moderate heat for about 30 minutes.
3. Add the rice to the cabbage mixture, and cook until almost tender, about 15 to 20 minutes. If the soup becomes too dry, add a little boiling water to it.
4. Stir in the cheeses and continue cooking for 5 minutes. Remove from the heat and allow to stand for 5 more minutes before serving.

La

Minestra

di Pane

Ribollita

di Chef

Piero

Ferrini

•

*Chef Piero
Ferrini's
Tuscan Bread
and Vegetable
Soup*

6 servings

• This is the classic minestrone soup of Tuscany. Chef Piero notes that *cavolo nero* (black cabbage) really enhances the flavor of the soup. This is one of the vegetables not yet grown in the United States, but Italian farmers in the Napa Valley, who produce all of the raddicchio that we enjoy in this country, hope to cultivate this variety of cabbage in the near future.

1 large onion, coarsely chopped
2 zucchini, finely chopped
2 celery sticks, finely chopped
2 carrots, finely chopped
^{1}/2 head of cabbage, finely chopped
20 leaves of black cabbage, finely chopped
    (escarole may be substituted if desired)
2 peeled tomatoes, finely chopped
6 tablespoons of extra-virgin olive oil, plus a little extra
1 15 ^{1}/2-ounce can of *cannellini* beans or ^{1}/2 pound of dried beans
6 cups of Vegetable Broth (page 61)
salt and freshly ground pepper to taste
2 cloves of garlic
1 large loaf of slightly stale Italian bread, cut into ^{1}/2-inch slices
3 cloves garlic, peeled and halved

1. If using dried beans, soak overnight, drain, and boil them in fresh water until tender (1 hour).
2. Put half of the onion and all of the vegetables in a large stockpot. Add 3 to 4 tablespoons of olive oil and cook until golden.
3. Add half the beans, purée the rest, and add them to the pot along with the Vegetable Broth. Season with salt and pepper, and cook for 1 ^{1}/2 hours.

74

4. Sauté the rest of the onion and the garlic in 2 tablespoons of olive oil and add to the soup. Stir well.
5. Toast the bread slices and rub with the cut side of garlic cloves and arrange one layer of these toasts in the bottom of a large Dutch oven.
6. Pour a generous ladleful of soup over the bread, then sprinkle on a little olive oil and ground pepper. Continue to layer the bread and soup in this way until the soup is used up. Let it sit for at least one hour or refrigerate overnight.
7. Before serving, boil the bread-soup mixture, stirring well, and serve. Each portion should be drizzled with additional extra-virgin olive oil.

*Tuscan
Pasta and
Bean Soup*

*5 to 6
servings*

• Though its origins are in Tuscany, this hearty soup is served in homes and restaurants all over Italy. This is Chef Piero Ferrini's wonderful recipe from Peggy Markel's cooking program, *La Cucina al Focolare*, at the 13th Century *Fattoria degli Usignoli* (Farm of the Nightingales) in Reggello, Tuscany.

1 onion finely chopped
2 cloves of garlic, finely minced
4 tablespoons of extra-virgin olive oil
1 1/2 cans (15 1/2-ounce size) of cannellini beans, drained or
      1 pound of dried *cannellini* beans
2 tablespoons of tomato paste
2 small potatoes, peeled and diced small
salt and freshly ground pepper to taste
2 or more cups of water or Vegetable Broth (page 61)
1 sprig of fresh rosemary
5 fresh sage leaves, chopped
1 cup of small pasta, such as *ditalini*, cooked in water and drained (reserve
      1 cup of the pasta-cooking water to add to the soup if necessary)

1. If using dried beans, soak them overnight, drain, cover with fresh water, and boil for 1 hour.
2. In a medium stock pot, sauté the onion and garlic in the olive oil, over medium heat, until golden brown.
3. Add the beans, tomato paste, and potatoes. Salt and pepper to taste.
4. Cover the bean mixture with water or broth, stir, and bring to a boil. Add the rosemary and sage. Lower heat and simmer until beans are tender (about 45 minutes to 1 hour). Add water when necessary to prevent sticking. Remove the sprig of rosemary and let the soup cool for 5 to 10 minutes.
5. Transfer the soup to a food processor and purée.

6. Return the soup to the stock pot. Add cooked pasta if desired, and some of the pasta water if the soup is too thick. Heat for about 5 minutes.
7. Ladle into individual soup bowls and drizzle generously with olive oil before serving.

TIP   Serve with crusty fresh bread. For a fancier bread, cut open a loaf of Italian bread (flat pizza bread is excellent for this) and drizzle it with extra-virgin olive oil, crushed rosemary leaves, and freshly ground pepper; bake in a hot (400-degree) oven until golden (about 8 minutes).

Conchigliette con Ceci e Domodoro

•

Tiny Shell Pasta with Tomato and Chick Pea Soup

4 to 5 servings as a first course

• A very easy soup to prepare, the rosemary seasoning makes it quite flavorful. This soup really is a meal in a dish because of the complex carbohydrates provided by the pasta and beans.

4 tablespoons of olive oil (preferably extra-virgin)
2 garlic cloves, finely chopped
1 28-ounce can of crushed plum tomatoes with their juices
1 tablespoon of fresh rosemary leaves, chopped
2 tablespoons of fresh Italian flat-leaf parsley, chopped
salt and freshly ground pepper to taste
1 15 1/2-ounce can of *ceci* beans (chick peas) or 1/2 pound of dried beans
1/2 pound of small pasta (*conchigliette or ditalini*)
1 cup of freshly grated Parmesan cheese

1. If using dried beans, pre-soak, drain, and then boil them in fresh water until tender (about an hour).
2. Heat the oil in a medium saucepan. Add the garlic and sauté gently until translucent. Add the crushed tomatoes, rosemary, and parsley. Season with salt and several grindings of pepper. Simmer, uncovered, for 15 to 20 minutes. Rinse the beans and add 2/3 of them to tomato sauce.
3. Place the other third of the beans in a blender or food processor. Blend until smooth, and then stir them into the tomato-and-bean soup. Cook for 10 minutes longer.
4. Bring 3 to 4 quarts of salted water to a boil in a medium saucepan. Add the pasta. Cook, uncovered, until the pasta is tender but still firm to the bite. Drain the pasta and add it to the soup. Taste and correct the seasoning. Serve with a generous sprinkling of Parmesan cheese and a few drops of good olive oil if you wish.

78

Primi Piatti: Pasta

Chef Enrico Franzese, Luna Convento Hotel, Amalfi

RECIPES

- *Linguine alla Bella Donna di Chef Enrico Franzese*
  CHEF ENRICO'S "LOVELY LADY'S LINGUINE"

- *Farfalle alla Marinara*
  BUTTERFLY PASTA WITH QUICK SAUCE

- *Spaghettini agli Asparagi e Pomodori*
  THIN SPAGHETTI WITH ASPARAGUS AND PLUM TOMATOES

- *Pennette ai Peperoni, Broccoli e Pinoli*
  QUILL PASTA WITH RED AND YELLOW PEPPERS, BROCCOLI FLORETS, AND PINE NUTS

- *Rotelle con Broccoli e Pesto*
  CORKSCREW PASTA WITH BROCCOLI AND PESTO

- *Fusilli alla Primavera*
  CURLY PASTA WITH SPRING VEGETABLES

- *Trenette al Pesto, Fagiolini e Patate*
  LONG, FLAT, THIN PASTA WITH PESTO, GREEN BEANS, AND POTATOES

- *Bucatini con Zucchine e Cipolle*
  BUCATINI WITH FRIED ZUCCHINI AND ONIONS

- *Ditalini ai Piselli e Pomodori*
  SMALL THIMBLE PASTA WITH PEAS AND PLUM TOMATOES

- *Rigatoni alla Norma*
  RIGATONI WITH FRIED EGGPLANT AND RICOTTA SALATA

- *Conchiglie con Cavolfiore all'Aglio e Olio e Peperoncini*
  FLUTED SHELL PASTA WITH CAULIFLOWER, OIL, GARLIC, AND HOT PEPPER

- *Paglia e Fieno*
  HAY AND STRAW—GREEN AND WHITE FETTUCCINE WITH
  SHALLOTS, MUSHROOMS, PEAS, AND CREAM

- *Orecchiette con Broccoli di Rape*
  LITTLE EAR PASTA WITH BROCCOLI RABE

- *Pappardelle con Salsa alle Verdure*
  WIDE RIBBON PASTA WITH HEARTY VEGETABLE SAUCE

- *Tagliatelle al Limone*
  TAGLIATELLE WITH LEMON-CREAM SAUCE

*P*ASTA HAS BEEN an integral part of Italian cuisine for centuries. There is evidence that many ancient conquerors of Italy enjoyed the first types of flour-and-water pastas much as we enjoy them today: the Arabs introduced strips of dough, or *trii*, to Sicily; the Greeks, *laganono* or *lasanon*; and the Romans, *lagano*. Even the Etruscan tombs, decorated with scenes from their homes, depicted a rolling pin and an indented wheel for pasta. In the Middle Ages, pasta shapes progressed from the wide variety of lasagna-type noodles to smaller shapes formed by rolling the dough around thin metal tubes, leaving holes, which enabled the pasta to cook better in broths and sauces. These shapes became the first examples of macaroni. As the years went on, a myriad of shapes of pasta developed, from fettuccine to tortellini and ravioli, the wonderful stuffed pastas of Emilia-Romagna. By the time of Marco Polo, dried pasta was already established in the cuisine of Italy.

The combination of tomatoes and pasta is associated with Naples. There are colorful lithographs from the 1800's showing Neapolitan *lazzaroni* (street kids) eating long spaghetti-like pasta by lowering it into their mouths with their fingers!

Perhaps pasta was introduced to America in the eighteenth-century, when Thomas Jefferson brought back a pasta press from his visit to Italy, inspiring the fame of "macaroni" from the well-known ditty, "Yankee Doodle Dandy." No matter when pasta actually arrived in America, the popularity of this beloved dish of the Italians has grown by leaps and bounds. Certainly the influx of Italian immigrants to the United States in the early 1900's spread the gospel of this healthy and comforting food.

In our extended Sicilian family, pasta was much more present in our daily meals than *risotto*, *gnocchi*, or *polenta*. While I do have childhood memories of Grandma Peppina drying her homemade *tagliatelle* and *fettuccine* on clean white cloths before the Sunday family dinner, mostly I remember eating *pasta secca*—commercially dried pasta in all shapes and sizes, served with a variety of sauces, from the traditional tomato-meat ragù to all types of vegetarian sauces.

My Grandpa Tony ate pasta every day of his 84 years. My mother, Frances, oldest of five daughters also required her *puntina di pasta* (little bit of pasta) every day. On the rare occasions when my mother made a roast for Sunday dinner, instead of the baked *rigatoni al ragù* that we came to expect every week, my younger sister, Frani, cried at its absence! We were all addicted to pasta, and we still are.

Americans use the generic word "pasta" to describe all types of this delicious, nutritious food. In my family we refer to the homemade egg, flour, and water variety as "fresh pasta," and the short, dried, commercially produced semolina flour variety, made from durum wheat and water, as "macaroni."

In general, fresh, long varieties of various widths are best served with light sauces and cream sauces. Short, open pasta (macaroni) is ideal with chunky sauces, especially vegetable- and tomato-based sauces, because the ridges and curved shapes trap and hold the sauce so well. Tiny pasta shapes are excellent in broths and cook very quickly. However, the pasta must be boiled first, drained, and then added to the broth, except for *pastina* and *capelli d'angelo* (angel hair). If you don't take this preliminary step, and instead put the pasta "raw" into the broth to cook, the broth will become cloudy and thick from the pasta's excess starch.

Dried pasta is produced in many of the regions of Italy and, fortunately, widely exported to the United States. I prefer cooking with this imported pasta. Italy's standards for making pasta are especially high because it is an economically important export for Italy.

Italians have two very strict rules about pasta: it must be cooked *al dente*, (with a little hard quality to the bite), and it must be served piping hot. I was amused several years ago when my husband and I were visiting Signora Ada Zambelli in Florence. I consider Signora Ada my "Italian Mama" when I am in Italy. She would not put the spaghetti in to boil until we were *a tavola* (at the table). How like my own mother, who would become incensed if all four of her daughters were not seated at the table when she served the steaming bowls of pasta!

TIPS FOR COOKING PERFECT
AL DENTE PASTA

I offer these simple tips for cooking perfect *al dente* pasta: Cook 1 pound of pasta in no less than 5 quarts (preferably 6 quarts) of briskly boiling water, to which 2 tablespoons of salt have been added. Some cooks prefer to add the salt after the water has come to a boil, but I am always fearful that I will forget to add it, especially if I am preparing several dishes at once. People who must avoid salt for health reasons should of course do so, but I'll have to say that pasta without salt can be rather bland and tasteless, although spicy sauces do help. No oil should be added to the water, as it will cause the sauce to slide off the pasta. The abundant water will prevent the individual pasta strands or macaroni from sticking. It is important to stir often.

The length of time required to cook the pasta will depend on the type of pasta used: fresh pasta needs just 2 to 3 minutes of cooking, while dried pasta may take 7 to 11 minutes to cook. The best way to check whether the pasta is *al dente* is to taste a strand or an individual macaroni. Do not throw it against a tiled wall to see if it sticks! When it is ready, drain the pasta in a large colander, with a bowl beneath it to capture some of the cooking water. This is especially important for many of the *pasta asciutta*, or dry sauce, recipes—those without broth. Many vegetable sauces require the addition of 1/2 to 1 cup of cooking liquid after the pasta has been sauced.

Once cooked, immediately put the drained pasta into a warmed serving bowl and toss it with the sauce. Do not rinse pasta before adding sauce, as this will cool down the pasta. You needn't rinse off the excess starch if you have cooked the pasta in enough water. Serve the pasta immediately after saucing, except in the case of *al forno* recipes, which are baked to completion in the oven. In those recipes, drain the pasta a few minutes before it reaches the *al dente* stage, as it will continue to cook in the oven. Overcooked, mushy pasta is a disaster!

VARIETIES OF PASTA

Bucatini: thicker than spaghetti and similar to *perciatelli,* the strands have a hole *(buca)* that runs the length of the pasta and makes a whistling sound as it is sucked into the mouth.

Capellini: very thin, like the strands of hair. *Capelli d'angelo* (angel hair) is the thinnest.

Cappelletti: "little hats" are small dumplings with a variety of stuffings. They are often served in broth.

Conchiglie: shaped like sea shells, and excellent for vegetable sauces and soups with beans. *Conchigliette* are tiny shells.

Farfalle: small, butterfly-shaped pasta, sometimes referred to as "bowties."

Fettuccine: long, fresh, ribbon-like noodles about $1/8$"-$3/8$" wide, usually made with eggs. Good for delicate sauces and cream sauces as in the famous recipe Fettuccine all' Alfredo.

Fusilli: spiral spaghetti, or a similar corkscrew-shaped macaroni called *rotelle.*

Lasagne: very wide noodles, sometimes with a fluted edge; used in layered, baked dishes that contain ricotta cheese. Now these are also available in the no-cook variety. Simply soak for five minutes before assembling the lasagne.

Linguine and *tagliolini:* long, thin, flat versions of *fettuccine.*

Maccheroni (macaroni): a term used for all commercially made dried pasta, particularly cut shapes with holes and twists.

Orecchiette: "little ears" formed by pressing the thumb into a small piece of pasta dough.

Pappardelle: long, wide noodles resembling ribbons. Serve with rich vegetable and mushroom sauces.

Pastina: the tiniest pasta, it can be boiled directly in the broth; a perfect, nutritious dish for babies.

Penne: short, tubular pasta cut in slashes on the diagonal, these are sometimes described as "quills." *Pennette* are thinner or shorter versions of *penne*. Both are made either ridged *(rigati)* or smooth *(lisce)*.

Ravioli: square-shaped, and sometimes round, individual dumplings, most often stuffed with a ricotta-spinach mixture. Many types of filling can also be used, such as puréed pumpkin or mushrooms.

Rigatoni: short, ridged, tubular macaroni used for rich, tomato-based sauces.

Spaghetti: the best-known variety of long, dried pasta. *Spaghettini* and *vermicelli* are thinner versions.

Tagliatelle: fresh, long, ¼-inch pasta, sometimes made with spinach added to the pasta dough, in which case it is called *tagliatelle verdi* (green *tagliatelle*).

Tortellini and *tortelloni:* small and large (respectively) dumplings with various stuffings, served in broths or with rich cream sauces.

Trenette: a somewhat narrower version of *fettuccine*, from Genoa; traditionally served with the famous *pesto allo genovese* sauce (page 95).

Tubetti and *tubettini:* regular-size and small thimble or tubular macaroni, served with peas and in soups with beans. *Tubettini* are delicious in clear broths.

Ziti: thinner, longer versions of the tubular *rigatoni* pasta, often used with thick ragù sauces and oven-baked *(al forno)* pasta dishes.

• Chef Enrico Franzese of the Luna Convento Cooking School in Amalfi taught us this version of the well-known *Puttanesca* sauce, which uses the same ingredients but adds spicy anchovies and hot pepper. Even the name *Bella Donna—Lovely Lady*—is gentler than the other version, which signifies a "lady of the night"!

1 pound of linguine
2 tablespoons of salt
2 cloves of garlic, minced
2 tablespoons of olive oil (preferably extra-virgin)
2 ounces of salted capers, rinsed and drained
4 ounces of black olives, pitted and chopped *(Gaeta* or *Kalamata)*
1 pound of chopped fresh tomatoes or 1 $^{1}/_{2}$ cups
    of canned crushed tomatoes
2 tablespoons of Italian flat-leaf parsley, chopped,
    plus additional parsley for garnish

1. Cook the linguine in 6 quarts of boiling water, to which 2 tablespoons of salt has been added, until *al dente.*
2. Meanwhile, in a large skillet sauté the garlic in the olive oil until golden, being careful not to burn it. Add the capers, black olives, chopped tomatoes, and parsley. Simmer for 5 to 7 minutes.
3. Drain the linguine and put it in the skillet containing the sauce. Toss and serve immediately, very hot, with additional parsley for garnish.

Chef Enrico's "Lovely Lady's Linguine"

5 servings as a first course

*Farfalle
alla
Marinara*

•

*Butterfly
Pasta with
Quick Sauce*

*5 servings
as a first
course*

• Our family gave this delicious sauce its nickname "quick sauce" because it can be prepared so quickly. As a variation, the sauce is excellent served over any type of long pasta (linguine, spaghetti, capellini), as well as short macaroni. For a heartier version of this dish, add 8 ounces of cubed fresh mozzarella and one small diced, sautéed eggplant after the pasta has drained. Always use fresh basil in making this sauce.

3 whole cloves of garlic
3 tablespoons of olive oil (preferably extra-virgin)
1 large can of Italian plum tomatoes or 1 28-ounce
    can of recipe-ready crushed tomatoes
2 teaspoons of dried oregano (optional)
salt and freshly ground pepper to taste
2 tablespoons of Italian flat-leaf parsley, minced
3 to 4 fresh basil leaves, slivered
1 pound of *farfalle* pasta
grated Parmesan cheese

1. In a 10 or 12-inch open skillet, sauté the garlic in the olive oil over medium heat until just golden (being careful not to burn it); discard the garlic.
2. Remove the pan from the flame. Put the plum tomatoes into the pan and break them coarsely with a fork (or add crushed tomatoes, if using them).
3. Add seasonings and herbs and return to low heat, simmering for 20 minutes.
4. Meanwhile, bring 6 quarts of water, to which 2 tablespoons of salt has been added, to a boil. Add the pasta, stir, bring back to a boil, and cook according to package directions (about 11 minutes for *farfalle*), or until *al dente*.

5. Drain the pasta and immediately put it in a warmed serving dish with half the sauce, and toss. Add the remaining sauce and serve immediately. Pass grated Parmesan cheese separately.

Tips   This sauce can be used in many other recipes, such as *Eggplant Parmigiana* (page 158), *Rigatoni alla Norma* (page 98), and Pizza (Chapter 8). For more intense garlic flavor, the garlic cloves may be minced and left in the sauce.

Spaghettini agli Asparagi e Pomodori

●

Thin Spaghetti with Asparagus and Plum Tomatoes

5 to 6 servings as a first course

● My mother created this recipe which is best made in the spring when fresh asparagus are tender and in great abundance in the markets. Very easy to prepare, it is a favorite in my cooking school.

4 to 5 scallions, cut into 1 1/2-inch diagonal pieces
3 tablespoons of olive oil (preferably extra-virgin)
2 cups of fresh or canned plum tomatoes , chopped
1 8-ounce can of tomato purée (optional)
salt and freshly ground pepper to taste
2 tablespoons of fresh basil leaves, torn
1 1/2 pounds of fresh asparagus, bottoms snapped off,
    sides scraped, and cut in 1 1/2-inch diagonal pieces
1 pound of spaghettini
2 tablespoons of Italian flat-leaf parsley, minced
1/2 cup of freshly grated Parmesan cheese

1. In a large open skillet, sauté the scallions in olive oil until soft.
2. Add plum tomatoes and tomato purée (if desired), salt, pepper, and basil. Simmer on low heat for 10 minutes.
3. Place the asparagus pieces in an open 10-inch skillet and cover with salted water. Bring to a boil and cook for 3 to 5 minutes. Drain and add to tomato sauce, and simmer for 5 to 7 minutes. (Add 1/2 cup of water if necessary.)
4. Meanwhile, bring 6 quarts of water, to which 2 tablespoons of salt has been added, to a boil. Add the spaghettini, stir, bring back to a boil, and cook according to package directions (about 5 to 7 minutes, or until *al dente*).
5. Drain the spaghettini, reserving 1 cup of the cooking water, and toss it with the sauce in a large, warmed platter. If necessary, add a little of the reserved cooking liquid from the pasta.
6. Sprinkle with parsley and serve immediately; pass the grated Parmesan cheese separately.

• This lovely, colorful dish is one of the few pasta dishes that I do not always serve piping hot. Try serving it at room temperature as part of a buffet, in place of a salad.

4 tablespoons of extra-virgin olive oil
1 medium onion, slivered
2 cloves of garlic, minced
1 $1/2$ pounds of sweet red and yellow peppers, seeded and
    cut into 3-inch strips
1 head of fresh broccoli, stems discarded, washed and cut into florets
salt and freshly ground pepper to taste
1 pound of *penne* or *pennette* pasta
flat-leaf Italian parsley, chopped
3 tablespoons of toasted *pinoli* nuts (optional; see below for
    toasting instructions)

1. Heat the olive oil in a large skillet, then add the onion and garlic and sauté over medium heat for 2 minutes. Add the peppers and broccoli and cook, covered, for 10 minutes, stirring every few minutes. Remove the lid, stir well, and cook for another 5 minutes. Add salt and pepper to taste.
2. Meanwhile, bring 6 quarts of water, to which 2 tablespoons of salt has been added, to a boil, and cook the *penne* according to package directions until *al dente*. Drain. Reserve $1/2$ cup of the pasta cooking water.
3. Turn the pasta into a heated serving bowl, stir in the onion, pepper, and broccoli mixture, and the reserved water if desired, and add the chopped parsley. Sprinkle with *pinoli* nuts if desired. Serve hot or at room temperature.

NOTE To toast *pinoli* nuts, place them on the oven tray of a toaster-oven or a regular oven, and bake at 350 degrees until golden—about 5 to 7 minutes.

Pennette ai Peperoni, Broccoli e Pinoli

•

Quill Pasta with Red and Yellow Peppers, Broccoli Florets, and Pine Nuts

6 to 8 servings

Rotelle

con

Broccoli e

Pesto

•

*Corkscrew
Pasta with
Broccoli
and Pesto*

*6 to 8
servings*

• Pesto sauce means summer to me. My children love this dish so much that I make a year's supply of pesto from our garden from June until August and freeze it in small containers. These containers disappear from time to time when my daughter visits from her New York apartment or my son returns to college after holiday vacations!

PESTO (BASIL) SAUCE:

2 cups of fresh basil leaves (if the leaves are large, tear into pieces)
2 tablespoons of pine nuts
2 to 3 cloves of garlic
salt to taste
$^1/_2$ cup of grated Parmesan cheese
3 tablespoons of grated Romano cheese
$^1/_2$ to $^3/_4$ cup of olive oil (half olive oil and half extra-virgin)

1. Put all of the ingredients in a food processor bowl except for the olive oil. Process until the consistency is pasty, scraping the bowl occasionally.
2. Pour $^1/_2$ cup olive oil through the feed tube of the processor until all is evenly mixed, add the remaining $^1/_4$ cup oil if a more liquid consistency is desired.

ROTELLE AND BROCCOLI

1 pound of *rotelle* pasta (or *conchiglie* shells)
1 head of fresh broccoli separated into florets
3 tablespoons of butter (optional)

1. Boil the *rotelle* in 6 quarts of boiling water, to which 2 tablespoons of salt has been added, until *al dente* (about 7 to 11 minutes). Add the broccoli 5 minutes before the pasta is cooked.
2. Drain the pasta and broccoli and transfer to a warmed dish. Toss with butter, if desired.
3. Add the pesto sauce, toss well and serve hot or at room temperature.

Fusilli alla Primavera

•

*Curly Pasta
with Spring
Vegetables*

*5 to 6
servings*

• *Primavera* means "springtime" in Italian, and spring offers many wonderful fresh vegetables. Don't hesitate to substitute your favorite fresh vegetables for those in the recipe below—for example, broccoli, mushrooms, or red and yellow peppers. For a slightly richer texture and flavor, a little cream may be added in Step 2 of the recipe.

1 pound of *fusilli* pasta (*rotelle* or *fettuccine* may be substituted)
2 tablespoons of butter (optional)
4 tablespoons of extra-virgin olive oil
1 small onion, slivered or 4 scallions, cut into 1 ¹/₂-inch pieces
    on the diagonal
6 or 7 asparagus, bottoms snapped off, scraped and cut into 1 ¹/₂-inch pieces
1 cup fresh or frozen tiny peas
2 small to medium fresh zucchini, sliced thin
3 or 4 fresh plum tomatoes, cut into ¹/₂-inch slices
salt and freshly ground pepper to taste
5 to 6 fresh basil leaves, torn
1 18-ounce can of tomato sauce or purée
2 tablespoons of fresh Italian flat-leaf parsley, minced

1. Bring 6 quarts of water, to which 2 tablespoons of salt has been added, to a boil and cook the *fusilli* according to package directions (about 7 to 11 minutes). Drain the pasta, reserving 1 cup of the cooking water. Toss with butter if desired. Transfer to a warmed serving platter.
2. Sauté onion or scallions in olive oil for about 3 minutes. When golden, add asparagus, peas, and zucchini; after 3 or 4 minutes, add sliced plum tomatoes.
3. Season with salt, pepper, and basil, and add the tomato sauce. Simmer until vegetables are tender yet still a little firm (5 to 7 minutes).
4. Gently spoon the *primavera* sauce on top of the pasta. Add the reserved water if needed. Sprinkle with chopped parsley and serve.

94

• Pesto sauce is now familiar to most Americans. In Genoa, where pesto sauce originated, the classic practice is to mix pasta, tiny string beans, and potatoes with the pesto.

> $^1/_2$ pound of small green string beans, stem end removed,
>   cut into 2-inch lengths
> 2 medium potatoes, peeled and cut into small dice
> 1 pound of *trenette* pasta (or *linguine* or *spaghettini*)
> 1 recipe of Pesto Sauce (page 92)

1. Bring 6 quarts of water, to which 2 tablespoons of salt has been added, to a boil in a large pot, and add the beans and potatoes. Bring back to a boil and cook for 5 minutes.
2. Add the *trenette*. Cook according to the package directions for dry pasta, or cook for 3 to 4 minutes for fresh pasta.
3. Drain the *trenette* and vegetables, reserving $^1/_4$ cup of the cooking water. Dilute the pesto with about 2 tablespoons of cooking water. Put the *trenette* and vegetables into a large warmed serving bowl, add the pesto, mix well, and serve immediately.

Trenette al Pesto, Fagiolini e Patate

•

Long, Flat, Thin Pasta with Pesto, Green Beans, and Potatoes

5 to 6 servings

Bucatini
with Fried
Zucchini
and Onions

5 to 6 servings
as a first course

• When I was 10 years old, my mother served this wonderful dish as a first course one night for dinner. We all loved it and asked why we had never had it before. She explained that it was my father's favorite pasta sauce, and that she hadn't been able to make it since his death three years before.

This is my sister Rosemary's absolute favorite pasta dish! It must be served with *bucatini*—the long, thick spaghetti with the hole in the center that whistles as you suck it into your mouth! Try it with grated Romano cheese, which has a sharper flavor than Parmesan.

6 tablespoons of extra-virgin olive oil
2 pounds of small zucchini, ends removed, sliced into $1/4$-inch rounds
1 medium onion, slivered
1 pound of *bucatini* pasta
1 cup of fresh basil leaves, torn into small pieces
salt and freshly ground pepper to taste
$1/2$ cup of freshly grated Parmesan or Romano cheese

1. Choose a sauté pan large enough to hold the zucchini in one layer. Add 4 tablespoons of the olive oil and turn the heat to medium high.
2. Add the zucchini and sauté, turning them over frequently until they become a light brown color on each side. Remove to a serving platter. Continue until all of the zucchini are sautéed.
3. In the remaining 2 tablespoons of olive oil, sauté the onion until almost golden. Add the onion and oil from skillet to the zucchini.
4. Cook the *bucatini* in 6 quarts of boiling water, to which 2 tablespoons of salt has been added, until *al dente* (about 10 to 11 minutes). Drain the pasta, reserving 1 cup of the cooking water.
5. Toss the pasta with the zucchini in the serving dish. Add basil, salt, pepper, and enough of the cooking water to moisten the pasta. Pass the grated Parmesan or Romano cheese separately.

• Quick and easy, and always possible to make with canned crushed tomatoes and frozen peas on hand. This recipe could also be a soup course.

2 cups of fresh or frozen peas
3 tablespoons of olive oil (preferably extra-virgin)
1 onion, finely chopped
2 cups of canned crushed plum tomatoes
salt and freshly ground pepper to taste
3 fresh basil leaves, torn
$^1/_2$ pound of *ditalini* or tiny pasta shells
$^1/_2$ cup of freshly grated Parmesan cheese

1. Cook the frozen peas according to package directions, or steam fresh peas in $^1/_2$ cup of salted water until just tender (3 to 5 minutes). Drain and reserve.
2. In a separate saucepan, sauté the onion in the olive oil until translucent. Add tomatoes, salt, pepper, and basil, and simmer the sauce for 10 minutes.
3. Add the peas to the tomato sauce and simmer for 5 minutes.
4. Meanwhile, cook the pasta in 6 quarts of boiling water, to which 2 tablespoons of salt has been added, until *al dente* (about 7 to 10 minutes). Drain, reserving 1 cup of the cooking water.
5. Mix the pasta, peas, tomatoes, and reserved water. Serve in deep bowls, and pass the Parmesan cheese separately.

Ditalini ai Piselli e Pomodori

•

Small Thimble Pasta with Peas and Plum Tomatoes

4 to 5 servings as a first course

*Rigatoni
with Fried
Eggplant
and Ricotta
Salata*

*5 to 6
servings*

• This dish was named in honor of the Sicilian composer Bellini, for his opera "Norma." We were served *Rigatoni alla Norma* at *La Battiata*, a wonderful family-owned *ristorante* at the gates of the *Piazza Armerina* in Sicily. Hanging on a sign below the restaurant name was the phrase *Cucina Casalinga*, which means "homestyle cooking." This delighted me because it is also the name of my cooking school.

TOMATO SAUCE (CAN BE MADE AHEAD OF TIME):

1/4 cup of olive oil
1/2 onion, chopped
2 garlic cloves, minced
1 28-ounce can of crushed plum tomatoes
salt and freshly ground pepper to taste
4 basil leaves, torn

Heat the olive oil in a large saucepan, add the onion and garlic, and sauté until translucent. Add the tomatoes, salt, pepper, and basil and simmer for 20 to 25 minutes. Sauce can be made ahead and stored in the refrigerator for several days or in the freezer for six months.

PASTA AND EGGPLANT:

2 eggplants, thinly sliced
salt
2 cups or more of olive oil or vegetable oil
1 pound of *rigatoni* pasta
1 cup of grated Ricotta Salata or 1 cup of freshly grated Romano cheese

1. Sprinkle the eggplant with salt, weigh it down with a heavy pan, and let it stand for 30 minutes in a colander. Drain and pat thoroughly dry.
2. Pour the oil into a large, deep, heavy skillet and deep-fry the eggplant until it is golden on both sides. Drain well on paper towels and set aside.
3. Cook the pasta in 6 quarts of boiling water, to which 2 tablespoons of salt has been added, until *al dente* (about 7 to 10 minutes). Drain, and toss with the Tomato Sauce (recipe facing page). Top each serving with eggplant slices and some of the Ricotta Salata or Romano cheese. Pass additional grated cheese at the table.

Conchiglie

con

Cavolfiore

all'Aglio e

Olio e

Peperoncini

●

*Fluted Shell
Pasta with
Cauliflower,
Oil, Garlic, and
Hot Pepper*

*4 to 5 servings
as a first course*

● For a really Sicilian flavor, add 4 ounces of chopped, pitted black olives, such as *Gaeta*, to this dish. The combination of the crushed red pepper and the black olives makes it very spicy.

1 head of cauliflower
1 slice of white bread
1/2 cup of olive oil (preferably extra-virgin)
2 large cloves of garlic
crushed red pepper flakes, to taste
salt
1 pound of *conchiglie* or other short macaroni
2 tablespoons of Italian flat-leaf parsley, minced
1/2 cup of freshly grated Romano cheese

1. Remove all the leaves from the cauliflower and rinse in cold water.
2. Boil the whole cauliflower in 4 quarts of salted water. Place a piece of white bread on top of the cauliflower during cooking to absorb the strong odor. Cover the pot and cook until fork-tender but not mushy (about 20 minutes). Remove the bread and drain. Remove the tough core of the cauliflower.
3. Sauté the garlic cloves and red pepper flakes (if desired) in olive oil until golden, then remove the garlic cloves. For more intense flavor, mince the garlic cloves and do not remove them from the oil. Add the cauliflower to the oil, breaking it into small pieces with a fork and turning it to coat thoroughly with oil.
4. Add salt and cook on high heat for 3 to 4 minutes. Turn off heat.
5. Cook the macaroni in 6 quarts of boiling water, to which 2 tablespoons of salt has been added, until *al dente* (about 8 to 10 minutes). Drain, reserving 1/2 cup of the cooking water.
6. Toss the cauliflower with the pasta in a warm serving bowl. Add the reserved water if too dry. Top with the chopped parsley and serve at once, passing the grated Romano cheese separately.

• This "hay and straw" pasta dish is a classic, originally made with diced *prosciutto*. It is rich and creamy because both butter and heavy cream are used in the sauce.

2 tablespoons of shallots, finely chopped
8 ounces of fresh mushrooms, sliced
1 cup of tiny peas (fresh, or frozen and thawed)
1 tablespoon of olive oil (preferably extra-virgin)
2 tablespoons of butter
1 cup of heavy cream
1 pound of green and white fettuccine (8 ounces each, preferably fresh)
1 cup of grated Parmesan cheese, plus additional for topping
salt and freshly ground pepper to taste
pinch of nutmeg, freshly grated

1. In a very large skillet, sauté the shallots, mushrooms, and peas in butter and olive oil over medium heat for 2 to 3 minutes.
2. Add the cream and stir lightly.
3. Raise the heat and bring the mixture to a slow boil to thicken it slightly. Take the pan off the heat and set aside.
4. Cook the fettuccine in 5 to 6 quarts of boiling water, to which 2 tablespoons of salt has been added, just until *al dente*. The pasta will continue to cook in the sauce.
5. Drain the fettucine thoroughly and add it all at once to the sauce.
6. Turn the heat to medium and stir gently but thoroughly to coat the noodles with the cream mixture. Transfer to a heated serving platter.
7. Add the Parmesan cheese, and toss with two serving forks.
8. Add the salt and pepper, and a few grindings of nutmeg. Mix thoroughly and serve immediately. Pass additional Parmesan cheese.

Paglia e Fieno

•

Hay and Straw— Green and White Fettuccine with Shallots, Mushrooms, Peas, and Cream

5 to 6 servings as a first course

Orecchiette con Broccoli di Rape

•

*Little Ear
Pasta with
Broccoli Rabe*

*4 to 5
servings
as a first
course*

• *Orecchiette* are small macaroni, shaped like "little ears." Most often associated with Apulia, in the south of Italy, they are formed by pressing the thumb into small pieces of pasta dough, making the shape of an ear. *Broccoli di Rape* or *rapini* has the appearance of small broccoli florets on long stems. They are, in fact, part of the turnip family. Boiling the broccoli rabe before sautéing it in garlic and oil helps to reduce the bitterness of this vegetable. The addition of a pinch of hot chili pepper flakes really adds zest to this pasta dish. Broccoli rabe without the pasta is a very popular *contorno*, or side dish, in Italy.

2 pounds of broccoli rabe
$^{1}/_{2}$ cup of extra-virgin olive oil
3 cloves of garlic, whole (garlic may be minced for more intense flavor)
crushed hot pepper flakes (optional)
salt and freshly ground pepper, to taste
1 pound of *orecchiette* pasta
$^{1}/_{2}$ cup of grated Pecorino Romano cheese

1. Trim off the bottom half of the broccoli rabe stems and all of the large, tough leaves. Cut the remaining broccoli rabe into 2-inch lengths and wash well in a colander.
2. In a large saucepan, bring 3 to 4 quarts of salted water to a boil, and add the broccoli rabe. Cook covered for 5 minutes; drain, reserving the water.
3. In a large skillet (10 to 12-inch), sauté the garlic cloves or the minced garlic and hot pepper flakes (if desired) in the olive oil until the garlic becomes translucent. Add the broccoli rabe and sauté until tender (about 5 to 7 minutes). Add salt and pepper and a little of the reserved cooking water to the skillet if too dry. Remove the whole cloves of garlic, if used.

4. Meanwhile, bring 6 quarts of water, to which 2 tablespoons of salt has been added, to a boil. Add the *orecchiette* and boil according to package directions or until *al dente*, usually 5 to 8 minutes.
5. Drain the pasta, reserving 1 cup of the cooking water, and transfer to a warm serving platter. Add the broccoli rabe and some of the reserved cooking water and toss well. Serve immediately, passing grated Romano cheese separately.

*Pappar-
delle con
Salsa alle
Verdure*

•

*Wide Ribbon
Pasta with
Hearty
Vegetable
Sauce*

*6 to 8
servings*

• Chef Piero Ferrini of *La Cucina al Focolare* ("Cooking by the Fireside"), Peggy Markel's cooking school in the hills of Tuscany near Florence, presented this rich, hearty sauce in his classes. Not only delicious over pasta, it would also be wonderful served with polenta instead. I think of this sauce as the winter version of a *Pasta Primavera*.

1 red onion, finely chopped
4 tablespoons of extra-virgin olive oil
2 carrots, julienned
2 celery sticks, julienned
2 zucchini, ends removed, julienned
1 red pepper and one green pepper, seeded and julienned
1 medium eggplant, ends removed, julienned (see eggplant in
    The Italian Pantry in Chapter 2, p. 19)
5 fresh plum tomatoes, peeled and diced
8 ounces of crushed canned tomatoes
1 bunch of beet greens or Swiss Chard leaves, well washed
    and torn into 3-inch pieces
1 bunch of fresh basil leaves, torn
salt and freshly ground pepper to taste
1 pound of *pappardelle* or *tagliatelle* pasta
1 tablespoon of butter (optional)
1/2 cup of freshly grated Parmesan cheese
2 tablespoons of Italian flat leaf parsley, finely minced

1. Sauté the onion in the olive oil in a large sauté pan or Dutch oven.
2. Add all of the julienned vegetables to the onions a little at a time, stirring well. Cook for about 5 to 10 minutes until the vegetables begin to soften.

3. Add the fresh and the canned tomatoes, the beet greens or Swiss chard, along with the basil leaves.
4. Cook for 25 minutes at a low simmer, partially covered, stirring from time to time and adding water if the mixture begins to stick. Add salt and pepper to taste.
5. In the meantime, bring 6 quarts of water, to which 2 tablespoons of salt has been added, to a boil. Add the pasta, stir, and cook for approximately 4 to 5 minutes.
6. Drain the pasta, reserving 1 cup of the cooking water, and place in a large warm bowl. Add a tablespoon of butter if desired. Top with half the sauce and gently toss. Add the remaining sauce, a sprinkle of Parmesan cheese, and the parsley, and serve immediately. Pass additional grated cheese.

Tagliatelle al Limone

•

Tagliatelle with Lemon-Cream Sauce

6 servings

• The lemons that grow abundantly on the terraced cliffs of the Amalfi coast are a wonder to behold—very large and juicy! My students and I were often treated to this pasta dish while attending the Cooking School at the Sirenuse Hotel. Antonio Sersale, the director of the program, and his marvelous Chef, Alfonso Mazzacano, have graciously shared this special recipe with us.

4 tablespoons of butter
1 cup of heavy cream
grated zest of 2 medium, scrubbed lemons plus 3 tablespoons
    of fresh lemon juice
salt
1 1/4 pounds of *tagliatelle* or *tagliolini* (preferably fresh)
1/3 cup of Parmesan cheese, freshly grated
3 tablespoons of fresh Italian flat-leaf parsley, finely minced

1. In a large skillet with high sides, or a heat-proof casserole dish, melt the butter and stir in the cream. Add the lemon juice and lemon zest, salt to taste, and keep on low heat for 3 to 4 minutes. Remove from heat.
2. Cook the *tagliatelle* in 5 to 6 quarts of water, to which 2 tablespoons of salt has been added, stirring often. Cook pasta until *al dente* (3 to 4 minutes for fresh pasta; follow package directions for dried pasta, usually 7 to 11 minutes). Drain the pasta well.
3. Slide the pasta into the pan with the lemon-cream sauce. Mix well over medium heat for 2 to 3 minutes. Stir in the Parmesan and sprinkle with minced parsley before serving.

Primi Piatti: Risotti e Gnocchi

Tony and Fran in Mom's kitchen, 1994

RECIPES

- ## Risotto alla Milanese con Brodo di Verdura
  RISOTTO WITH VEGETABLE BROTH

- ## Risotto alla Primavera
  RISOTTO WITH SPRING VEGETABLES

- ## Risotto ai Funghi Porcini
  RISOTTO WITH PORCINI MUSHROOMS

- ## Risotto ai Carciofini e Pesto di Chef Enrico
  CHEF ENRICO'S RISOTTO WITH ARTICHOKES AND PESTO

- ## Risi e Bisi alla Veneziana
  RICE AND PEAS VENETIAN STYLE

- ## Farrotto con Peperoni
  FARROTTO WITH YELLOW AND RED PEPPERS

- ## Gnocchi Verdi di Mamma
  MOM'S SPINACH AND RICOTTA DUMPLINGS

- ## Gnocchi alla Sorrentina
  POTATO DUMPLINGS WITH TOMATO SAUCE, MOZZARELLA, AND PARMESAN CHEESE

- ## Gnocchi alla Romana
  SEMOLINA GNOCCHI BAKED WITH BUTTER AND PARMESAN CHEESE

ISOTTO, LONG A FAVORITE first course in Italy, has become recognized in America as the wonderful creamy, versatile dish that it has always been. To make a proper *risotto*, a special kind of rice produced in Italy must be used. *Arborio, carnaroli,* and *vialone* are the varieties (not brands) of choice. These short-grain varieties of rice have a starchiness that, with proper cooking, produces the rich, creamy texture of a perfect *risotto*—one that maintains an *al dente* firmness similar to that of perfectly cooked pasta. This result is virtually impossible to achieve with long-grain rice.

Most of Italy's rice comes from the regions of Piedmont, Lombardy, or Veneto. In the United States, it is found in Italian specialty stores and in some of our local supermarkets, in one-pound muslin sacks or in pressure-packed plastic bags (usually two pounds). *Arborio, carnaroli,* and *vialone* are more costly than native long-grain rice, but they are well worth the price. My son, Joe, adores *risotto* and requests it for his homecoming dinners and birthday celebrations.

I offer a few tips to help you prepare great *risotto* every time. Always choose a very heavy, large saucepan or Dutch oven. Make sure the broth or stock that you are adding to the rice is kept at a simmer. This will help in the proper absorption of the liquid by the rice. Be sure to use freshly grated, good-quality Parmesan cheese, (*Parmigiano-Reggiano* is the best).

The method of making *risotto* is almost always the same. Sauté a minced onion in the fat (butter or olive oil), just until translucent, then stir in the raw rice until it is well coated. Usually, a small amount of white wine ($1/2$ cup) is added. After waiting a few moments for the alcohol to evaporate, add the hot broth $1/2$ cup at a time, stirring constantly, until the *risotto* reaches the *al dente* stage.

Many different vegetables may be added during cooking, but the freshly grated Parmesan cheese is generally added at the very end. As an alternative to serving the *risotto* as a first course, any of the recipes in this chapter can be made into a *sformato*—a molded version of *risotto*, and a very dramatic presentation, perfect for a buffet.

There are basically three types of *gnocchi* in Italian cuisine, although you will find many variations of these, depending on the region where the recipe originated. Our family's favorite is my mother's recipe for *Gnocchi Verdi* (page 118)—tender, fluffy dumplings made of ricotta, spinach, flour, and egg, with a hint of nutmeg, and simply baked with butter and Parmesan cheese. In the south of Italy, along the Amalfi coast, the famous *Gnocchi di Patate alla Sorrentina* (page 120) are favored. I have observed chefs in Italy, from Tuscany to Amalfi, preparing *gnocchi*; some use no egg, and some use just the yolk, but my friend and assistant, Balbina Schiano, from the island of Ischia off the coast of Naples, has convinced me that adding the white of the egg as well as the yolk results in lighter *gnocchi*.

Most important, in making this type of *gnocchi*, is to be sure that the cooked potatoes you use are very dry before you put them through the ricer. If too moist, they will absorb too much flour and produce heavy dumplings—something akin to mushy pasta! Potato *gnocchi* are usually served with a tomato sauce and topped with grated Parmesan cheese, mozzarella, and basil, but they can also be served with a simple butter-and-Parmesan sauce with a hint of fresh sage.

Gnocchi alla Romana (page 122) are dumplings pressed out of a batter of semolina flour, milk, egg yolk, Parmesan cheese, and nutmeg. The mixture is allowed to set, after being spread on a flat pan, until it becomes firm; this is very much like the way you prepare *polenta*. Traditionally, the *gnocchi* are cut into 2-inch rounds and placed, overlapping, in an ovenproof serving dish to be topped with butter and Parmesan cheese, baked, and then placed under the broiler for the last few minutes to achieve a golden crust on top.

These semolina dumplings would be marvelous accompanied by a hearty ragù of vegetables like *Giambotta* (page 163) or *Salsa alle Verdure* (page 104). I think you will find that all the types of *gnocchi* described in this book will be a welcome addition to your *primi piatti* repertoire.

• The traditional *Risotto alla Milanese* uses beef bone marrow as the fat in which the rice is sautéed. This recipe uses butter in its place. The saffron gives the finished *risotto* a golden hue.

5 to 6 cups of Vegetable Broth (page 61)
4 tablespoons of unsalted butter
1 medium onion, minced
2 cups of Italian *arborio* rice
$^1/_8$ teaspoon of saffron, powdered or threads, diluted in 1 cup of the broth
salt and freshly ground pepper to taste
$^2/_3$ cup of freshly grated Parmesan cheese

1. Heat the broth in a three quart saucepan to a simmer.
2. In a large, heavy saucepan or Dutch oven, melt the butter over medium heat and sauté the onion until translucent (about 3 minutes). Add the rice, and stir until coated.
3. Add just enough broth to cover the rice (about $^1/_2$ cup). Stir well.
4. Cook the rice on medium heat, stirring constantly. As the broth is absorbed, add more (about $^1/_2$ cup at a time). When the rice has absorbed all 5 cups of broth, test for tenderness. If it is still hard, add additional half-cups of broth. Keep on stirring and cooking until tender but not mushy. (Total cooking time is about 18 to 22 minutes).
5. Stir in the saffron-broth mixture. When the rice is evenly colored and flavored by the saffron, stir in the grated Parmesan cheese. Taste again; when creamy yet *al dente*, remove from heat. Add salt and pepper to taste. Serve immediately.

*Risotto
with Spring
Vegetables*

*6 servings as
a first course,
3 to 4 as a
main course*

• This dish is lovely because of the bright colors of the vegetables with the creamy white rice. For a dramatic presentation, serve *risotto* molded by packing the cooked rice into a 3-quart bowl or mold. Let it stand for 3 minutes, cover the mold with a round serving plate, and invert. Lift off the mold and serve at once with more vegetables in the center or topped with a light tomato sauce.

2 tablespoons of extra-virgin olive oil
4 tablespoons of butter
$1/4$ pound of fresh mushrooms, wiped clean with a damp cloth
    and sliced thin
1 small zucchini, ends removed, sliced thin
$1/4$ pound of fresh asparagus, bottoms snapped off, scraped,
    and cut into 1-inch diagonal pieces
1 small red bell pepper, cored, seeded, and diced
$1/2$ cup of tiny peas (fresh, or frozen and thawed)
5 to 6 cups of Vegetable Broth (page 61)
1 medium yellow onion, finely diced or 3 shallots, finely minced
2 cups of *arborio* rice
salt and freshly ground pepper to taste
$2/3$ cup of freshly grated Parmesan cheese

1. In a 10-inch skillet, heat the olive oil and 2 tablespoons of the butter, and add the mushrooms. Sauté for 3 minutes. Add the zucchini, asparagus, red pepper, and peas, and sauté for 3 minutes. Remove from heat.
2. Heat the Vegetable Broth to a simmer in a 3-quart saucepan.
3. Heat the remaining 2 tablespoons of butter in a large heavy saucepan or Dutch oven. Add the onion or shallots, and sauté over medium heat until translucent. Add the rice and stir until well coated.

4. Add $^{1}/_{2}$ cup of the hot broth and cook, stirring constantly, until the liquid is almost absorbed. Continue adding broth, $^{1}/_{2}$ cup at a time, and stir constantly for about 15 minutes.
5. When the *risotto* has been cooking for about 15 minutes, add the vegetables to the rice. Stir well and continue to add the broth until the rice is tender yet firm to the bite (*al dente*)—about 7 to 10 minutes more. Add salt and pepper to taste.
6. Remove from heat; stir in Parmesan cheese and serve immediately.

Risotto
ai Funghi
Porcini

•

Risotto
with Porcini
Mushrooms

6 servings

• Porcini mushrooms have a very pungent, woodsy flavor. For a more delicate version, 8 ounces of cultivated mushrooms (sliced thinly) may be used instead of the porcinis. They should be sautéed briefly (3 minutes) in 3 tablespoons of butter or extra-virgin olive oil and added in Step 5 in place of porcinis.

5 to 6 cups of Vegetable Broth (page 61)
4 tablespoons of unsalted butter
1 medium yellow onion, finely chopped
2 cups of *arborio* rice
1 cup of dry white wine
1 ounce of dried porcini mushrooms, soaked in 1 cup
    of lukewarm water for 10 to 15 minutes
$1/8$ teaspoon of saffron, powdered or threads (optional)
salt and freshly ground pepper to taste
$2/3$ cup of freshly grated Parmesan cheese

1. Heat the broth in a three-quart saucepan to a simmer.
2. Sauté the onion in the butter in a large, heavy saucepan or Dutch oven until soft and translucent (about 3 minutes). Add the rice and stir until coated. Stir in the wine and cook until it evaporates (about 3 minutes).
3. Dissolve the saffron in 1 cup of the broth and set aside.
4. Add $1/2$ cup of broth and stir; repeat the process for about 10 minutes.
5. Drain the porcini, reserving the soaking liquid. Strain the liquid through two layers of cheese cloth to remove grit. Chop the porcini coarsely, and add to the rice along with the strained soaking liquid.
6. Stir in the saffron mixture, salt and pepper.
7. Continue adding broth and stirring after each addition for another 10 minutes or so, until the rice is *al dente*.
8. When the rice is evenly colored by the saffron, stir in the Parmesan cheese. Transfer to a warm serving bowl and serve immediately.

• Chef Enrico Franzese, of the Luna Convento Hotel Cooking School in Amalfi, created this dish for our "graduation" banquet. Enrico speaks no English, so I described in Italian the luscious consistency of the risotto: *come seta*—like silk—and he beamed!

> 1 package of frozen artichoke hearts (see note), thawed
> 2 cups of *arborio* rice
> 4 tablespoons of butter
> 5 to 6 cups of hot Vegetable Broth (page 61)
> salt and freshly ground pepper to taste
> $^1/_2$ cup of grated Parmesan cheese
> 2 to 3 tablespoons of Pesto Sauce (page 92, or purchased
>   fresh pesto may be substituted)

1. Cut artichoke hearts in half lengthwise, sauté in 2 tablespoons of the butter for 3 to 5 minutes, and set aside. (Cook longer if using fresh artichoke hearts: 5 to 8 minutes, covered.)

2. In a very heavy large saucepan or Dutch oven, sauté the rice in 2 tablespoons of the butter, stirring until the rice is coated with butter. Ladle in the simmering broth, $^1/_2$ cup at a time, stirring constantly. After 15 minutes, add the artichoke hearts. Continue adding broth until the liquid is used up and the rice is *al dente* (about 5 minutes longer). If the rice is still raw to the taste, continue adding broth or hot water until the consistency is creamy and rice is *al dente*.

3. Add the Parmesan cheese and the Pesto Sauce. Stir well and serve immediately with a sprinkling of chopped parsley on top.

NOTE   Fresh baby artichokes are difficult to find in the markets here. Since fresh ones are not often available, frozen artichoke hearts have been substituted in this recipe. If using fresh tiny artichokes, remove the stems and all the tough outer leaves. Cut into quarters and put in bowl of water to which the juice of one lemon has been added. When ready to sauté, drain, and pat dry with paper towels.

Risi e Bisi alla Veneziana

•

Rice and Peas Venetian Style

6 servings

• *Risi e Bisi* is a very popular dish in Venice and in the whole region surrounding that famous city of the Doges, who were said to have served it each April 25th for the feast of Saint Mark, the patron saint of the city. Considered by many as a soup, I have included it in this *Risotto* chapter since the thickness of the dish demands using a fork rather than a spoon to eat it.

1/4 cup of butter
1 tablespoon of olive oil (preferably extra-virgin)
1 small onion, chopped
2 tablespoons of chopped parsley
7 cups of Vegetable Broth (page 61)
2 1/2 cups of fresh peas, shelled, or frozen peas, thawed
salt
2 cups of *arborio* rice
2/3 cup of freshly grated Parmesan cheese
additional Parmesan cheese and fresh minced parsley for garnish

1. Melt 2 tablespoons of the butter with the olive oil in a large heavy saucepan or Dutch oven. When the butter foams, add the onion and parsley and sauté for 2 minutes over medium heat. Add the peas. If using fresh peas, add 3 cups of broth and salt to taste, and bring to a moderate boil for 10 minutes. If using thawed peas, add 1 cup of broth and salt, and cook for 2 to 3 minutes.
2. Meanwhile, bring the remaining broth to a boil in a medium saucepan.
3. Add the rice to the pea mixture, stir well, and add the remaining broth. Stir again and cover. Cook at a slow boil for 10 to 15 minutes, stirring occasionally, until the rice is tender but still *al dente* (firm to the bite).
4. Remove from the heat and stir in the remaining butter and the Parmesan cheese. Serve immediately with additional Parmesan cheese and a sprinkling of parsley.

• "This was for me the natural way to make a special dish when I first saw the crushed grains of *farro*: make it similar to when I make *risotto*. I called it *Farrotto*. I never knew that this was a very typical name already in some areas of Tuscany. This particular version I find wonderful, as it combines the sweetness of the peppers with the nuttiness of the *farro*."

—*Rolando Beramendi*

Farrotto with Yellow and Red Peppers

5 to 6 servings

1 quart of Vegetable Broth (page 61)
$^1/_2$ cup of extra-virgin olive oil plus extra for drizzling on top
1 small onion, chopped fine
$^1/_2$ pound of crushed *farro*
$^1/_2$ cup of dry white wine
1 pound of diced red and yellow bell peppers
salt and freshly ground pepper to taste
chopped Italian parsley for garnish

1. In a large pot, bring the broth to a boil.
2. In a separate pot of about the same size, heat the olive oil and sauté the onion until transparent. Add the crushed *farro*. Add the white wine and stir until absorbed. Add the pepper cubes and mix well. Add two ladles ($^1/_2$ - 1 cup each) of broth, and continue to stir. Once the broth evaporates, add another ladle of broth and continue to stir. Add salt and pepper to taste. Taste the *farrotto* after 15 minutes and check for consistency. It does not take as long as making a *risotto*, but the texture depends on how hot you cooked the *farrotto*.
3. Once it is according to your taste, add two ladles of broth and let it sit for a couple of minutes.
4. Serve topped with chopped parsley and a drizzle of olive oil.

Gnocchi

Verdi di

Mamma

•

Mom's
Spinach
and Ricotta
Dumplings

6 to 8
servings

• In Italian, these *gnocchi* are called *ravioli nudi* (without jackets) and *malfatti*, (badly made) because of their imperfect shape and somewhat ugly appearance. Those descriptions aside, they are fluffy and delicious and they disappear quickly when served!

> 1 10-ounce package of frozen chopped spinach,
>   thawed (for fresh spinach, see note below)
> 1 pound of whole-milk ricotta cheese
> 1 large egg
> 1/2 teaspoon of freshly grated nutmeg
> 1 scant teaspoon of salt
> 4 tablespoons of grated Parmesan cheese plus 3 more
>   for sprinkling on *gnocchi* before baking
> 3/4 cup of flour
> 8 tablespoons of unsalted butter

1. Barely cook the spinach or let it defrost at room temperature. Drain, pressing a spoon against the side of the strainer to remove as much moisture as possible. Mince finely.
2. Put the ricotta in a medium-size bowl, add the spinach, and mix well. Add the unbeaten egg, nutmeg, and salt; mix. Fold in the Parmesan cheese and 1/2 cup of the flour.
3. Put the remaining 1/4 cup of flour in a dish, and drop 1 teaspoonful of the spinach mixture into it at a time. Roll it around in the dish until a little ball is formed. Remove and place on a cookie sheet or tray that has been lined with wax paper. Repeat until all the spinach mixture is used up.

4. Bring 5 quarts of water to a boil; add 1 tablespoon of salt. Drop in the *gnocchi* one by one until they cover the bottom of the pot. When the *gnocchi* rise to the top, remove them carefully with a slotted spoon, shake off the water and, put in a buttered oven-proof dish. As you remove cooked *gnocchi*, add more uncooked *gnocchi* to the boiling water. When all the *gnocchi* are boiled and drained, dot them with the butter and sprinkle with the rest of the Parmesan cheese.
5. Bake in a 375-degree oven until heated through (about 8 to 10 minutes. Put under the broiler for 2 more minutes or until golden.

NOTE   Fresh spinach can be used in this recipe, but sometimes the consistency is not as good as the frozen chopped spinach. The fresh spinach can be stringy if all of the stems are not removed carefully and if it is not chopped finely.

*Potato
Dumplings
with
Tomato Sauce,
Mozzerella,
and Parmesan
Cheese*

*8 servings or
the recipe may
be halved to
serve 4 people*

• Potato *gnocchi* are tricky to make because of the consistency of the potatoes. If the potatoes are not dry enough, the *gnocchi* will absorb too much flour and become heavy. I find that adding the white of one egg makes lighter, fluffier *gnocchi*.

GNOCCHI:

2 1/2 pounds of potatoes (Idaho or russet)
3/4 pound of flour (approximately 2 1/2 cups)
1 egg plus 1 yolk

1. Cook the potatoes with the skin on and drain when tender; check at 30 minutes (Alternately, potatoes may be wrapped individually and baked in a 400-degree oven for 40 minutes.)
2. Remove potato skins and press through a ricer.
3. On a marble or wooden board, add the flour and eggs and work the dough until pliable.
4. Break off a 3-inch piece and work it on a table, making a long rope, a 1/2-inch thick. Cut into 1-inch pieces. Make an indentation in each of the *gnocchi* by gently pressing it against the tines of a fork.
5. Cook in batches in about 4 to 5 quarts of boiling, salted water. When the *gnocchi* pop to the top, they are ready to be drained and placed in an oven-proof dish.

TOMATO SAUCE:

1 to 2 cloves of garlic, chopped
3 tablespoons of olive oil (preferably extra-virgin)
1 1/2 pounds of fresh peeled tomatoes, puréed, or 1 28-ounce can
    of crushed plum tomatoes
3 basil leaves, shredded
salt and freshly ground pepper to taste

Sauté the garlic in the olive oil until golden. Add the tomatoes, basil, salt, and pepper, and simmer for approximately 20 minutes.

GARNISH:

8 ounces of mozzarella, cut in small cubes
6 fresh basil leaves, torn
$^1/_2$ cup of freshly grated Parmesan cheese

ASSEMBLY:

Pour the sauce over the gnocchi and sprinkle with the mozzarella, basil, and Parmesan. Bake in a 350-degree oven for 10 minutes. Serve immediately.

Gnocchi alla Romana

Semolina Gnocchi Baked with Butter and Parmesan Cheese

6 servings

● Semolina is the very fine yellow flour used to make dried pasta. The method of making the *gnocchi* dough is similar to the one used to make *polenta*. For *Gnocchi alla Romana*, milk is used instead of the water used in *polenta* recipes.

vegetable oil for greasing the baking sheet
3 cups of milk
1 ½ teaspoons of salt
a generous pinch of freshly ground nutmeg
a generous pinch of freshly ground black pepper
1 cup plus 2 tablespoons of semolina
2 large egg yolks, lightly beaten
1 cup of freshly grated Parmesan cheese (about 3 ounces)
6 tablespoons of butter

1. Line the bottom of a 15 ½- by 10 ½-by 1-inch baking pan with aluminum foil. Generously oil the foil.
2. Heat the milk, salt, nutmeg, and pepper in a heavy 3-quart saucepan over medium-high heat, just to simmering. Do not boil; reduce heat to medium-low. Begin whisking or stirring the milk mixture briskly and add the semolina in a thin, steady stream, taking care not to let lumps form. Cook, stirring frequently, until thick enough for a spoon to stand upright and un-supported in the center of the mixture (about 15 minutes). Reduce heat to low; continue cooking, stirring constantly, until very thick (about 5 minutes longer). Remove from heat.
3. Add egg yolks, 3/4 cup of the cheese, and 2 tablespoons of the butter to the semolina mixture; stir until the butter is melted and the mixture is smooth.

4. Transfer the semolina mixture to the prepared pan. Pat out with a wet spatula to 3/8-inch thick. Alternatively, cut a piece of wax paper the size of the pan and place it over the *gnocchi* dough. With palms of hands, press on the paper until the dough is evenly spread in the pan. Refrigerate uncovered until cold (at least 1 hour).

5. Preheat the oven to 400 degrees. Turn the dough out of the pan onto a flat surface; peel off the foil. Cut the *gnocchi* with a 2-inch round cutter (don't waste the scraps; put them in a separate casserole dish and bake). Arrange the *gnocchi*, overlapping, in a 10-inch, shallow, flameproof baking dish. Melt the remaining butter in a small saucepan. Drizzle the melted butter over the *gnocchi*; sprinkle with the remaining cheese. Bake until the tops of the *gnocchi* are crisp and golden (about 15 minutes). Place under broiler, about 4 inches from the heat, until light brown (1 to 2 minutes). Serve at once.

Pizze, Focaccie e Panini

RECIPES

- *Focaccia al Rosmarino*
  FOCACCIA WITH ROSEMARY

- *Impasto per Pizza e Focaccia*
  PIZZA AND FOCACCIA DOUGH

- *Pizza Margherita*
  TRADITIONAL NEAPOLITAN PIZZA WITH TOMATO SAUCE, MOZZARELLA, AND BASIL

- *Pizza con Pesto, Pomodoro, Mozzarella e Olive*
  PESTO PIZZA WITH PLUM TOMATOES, FRESH MOZZARELLA, AND BLACK OLIVES

- *Pizza Quattro Stagioni*
  FOUR-SEASONS PIZZA

- *Pizza alle Melanzane*
  SPICY EGGPLANT PIZZA

- *Calzone di Verdura alla Balbina*
  BALBINA'S VEGETABLE CALZONE

- *Schiacciata alle Cipolle*
  FLATBREAD WITH THINLY SLICED ONIONS

- *Zeppole di Grandpa Tony*
  GRANDPA TONY'S FRIED DOUGH

- *Pane Origanato*
  ITALIAN BREAD BAKED WITH EXTRA-VIRGIN OLIVE OIL AND OREGANO

- *Panini*
  LITTLE SANDWICHES

- *Sfincione di Grandpa Tony*
  GRANDPA TONY'S SICILIAN PIZZA

IT WASN'T UNTIL I was a 22-year-old college student, traveling to Italy for the first time, that I experienced the individual, light, simply prepared pizzas that I discovered there. At home, we almost always ate thick pizza, Sicilian style. My mother often made it for us as a snack after school or on Friday nights as a meatless dinner. But the pizza I remember best is the thick, fluffy *Sfincione* (page 146) that my Grandpa Tony, a baker, made on Sunday nights before we headed back to the Bronx.

In a Sunday ritual, the pizza dough would be rising when we arrived at noon to enjoy the family dinner together. Grandpa would partially uncover the bowl in which he had placed the dough and we would exclaim about how excited we were for his evening "snack." My grandparents were concerned that we not go home hungry, since the trip was a little over an hour from their home on Long Island to ours. Some Sunday nights, Grandpa divided the dough into small balls, stretched them just a bit into flat discs, and then deep-fried them. These were called *zeppole*, like those you eat at Italian feast-day fairs. He offered us three choices of toppings: sugar, salt, or pizza sauce. Incredibly delicious!

Most of the recipes in this chapter are based on the same basic dough recipe (page 130). After the second rising, you may choose to form the crust into one large rectangle or one large circular pizza or *focaccia*. The other option is to make individual pizzas, about 8-inches across. Individual pizzas are most often found in the *trattorie* and pizzerias of Italy, and are eaten with a knife and fork.

I offer two items besides pizza and *focaccia* in this chapter: *calzoni*, the savory stuffed trouser-leg-looking pizzas; and *panini*, the little sandwiches of Italy that can be made from *focaccia* or hard rolls. They are found in just about all the cafés and bars in Italy, and are also becoming a presence in restaurants in the United States.

One of the most delicious features of an excellent pizza is its crust, especially when baked in a brick, wood-fired oven. Because it is difficult to duplicate the crispy texture in our gas and electric ovens, I have included some tips for achieving the crispy crust in your home oven.

Once you become confident about making your own homemade pizza, you won't be as happy with the restaurant variety. Making pizza is a great family activity; children love to knead the dough, and everyone enjoys fixing an individual pizza with his or her own selection of favorite toppings. A pizza party is a great theme for birthday celebrations—for all ages! Over the years, my pizza classes are always sold out. Grandpa Tony knew what he was doing on those Sunday nights; like the song says, "When the moon hits your eye like a big pizza pie, that's *Amore*"—the special ingredient he baked into every pizza!

BAKING TIPS FOR BREADS AND PIZZAS

1. In an electric oven, place the pizza on the lowest rack for better browning of the crust. In a gas oven, the pizza can be baked on the floor of the oven on a pizza stone or on tiles (pre-heated).
2. If possible, use a perforated pizza pan (one with holes in the bottom). This will make your crust crispier.
3. Sprinkle cornmeal on the pizza pan before spreading the dough for a crispy crust, and also to prevent the crust from sticking to the pan.
4. About 5 minutes after putting the pizza in the oven, spray the oven with water, or throw 4 to 6 ice cubes toward the back and floor of the oven, being careful not to land the cubes on the dough itself. The steam from the water or ice in the hot oven results in a crispier crust.

Safety Tips for Making Pizza

1. Pizzas are baked at very high temperatures (450 to 475 degrees). Therefore, special care should be taken when removing the pizza from such a hot oven: always use oven mitts, not pot holders, to protect your lower arm from a steam burn; open the oven and wait a minute before reaching in to remove the pizza, allowing the steam to escape without its flowing directly into your face.
2. If possible, buy a pizza pan that comes with a heat-proof carrier tray. This can go right on the table and makes cutting the hot pizza easier.

• This simple Italian flatbread derives its name from the Latin word *focus*, meaning "hearth," because the dough was formed on a stone slab and baked on the hearth. It is delicious topped with sun-dried tomatoes, roasted peppers, or eggplant *caponata*. To make *panini* (little sandwiches), cut the *focaccia* in squares, slit them in half, and stuff with cheeses and roasted vegetables.

1 Focaccia Dough (page 130)
cornmeal for sprinkling on the pan
3 to 4 tablespoons of extra-virgin olive oil
3 tablespoons of rosemary leaves (fresh or dried)
freshly ground pepper
kosher or coarse sea salt (optional)

1. Let the Focaccia Dough rise in an oiled bowl covered with a clean towel for about 1 hour; punch it down and let it rise again.
2. Preheat the oven to 450 degrees.
3. After the second rising, punch the dough down. Stretch the dough with your hands and pat it into a 16-inch round pizza pan, or an 11 by 16-inch rectangular pan that has been sprinkled lightly with cornmeal.
4. Press your fingers into the dough, creating a dimpling effect. Drizzle the olive oil over the dough, sprinkle it with the rosemary, pepper, and salt, if desired.
5. Bake on the lowest oven rack for 15 to 20 minutes, or until golden. For a crispy crust, see Baking Tips for Breads and Pizzas, page 128.

Focaccia al Rosmarino

•

Focaccia with Rosemary

10 to 12 servings

*Pizza and
Focaccia
Dough*

*1 large 16-inch
round or
rectangular
pizza shell, or
4 individual
pizza shells.*

• Making homemade pizza dough is always a satisfying culinary experience. I know that the results will be something special for me and my family. Children especially love working with dough, and should be allowed to help. The pizza classes in my "Kids Cook Italian" series are always full!

1 ¹/₂ cups of very warm (not hot) water
1 package of dry yeast
1 tablespoon of granulated sugar
3 ³/₄ cups of unbleached flour plus a little extra for
       kneading on the board
1 ¹/₂ teaspoons of salt
2 tablespoons of olive oil plus 1 tablespoon for coating
       the mixing bowl

In a large measuring cup, combine the water, yeast, and sugar. Leave for 10 minutes or until foamy. If the mixture does not rise, throw it away and use a new package of yeast.

FOOD PROCESSOR METHOD:

1. While the yeast is "proofing," combine the flour and salt in the bowl of a food processor. Pulse two or three times with the plastic dough blade. (The metal blade can also be used, but if children are using the processor, I suggest that only the plastic dough blade be used; removing the dough from the workbowl can involve touching the blade, which is very sharp.)

2. When the yeast-and-water mixture is foamy, turn the food processor on and pour the yeast mixture through the feed tube until the dough pulls away from the sides of the bowl. If the dough does not form a ball, add more flour by tablespoons until the dough forms a ball.

3. Continue to process for 45 seconds to a minute. Turn off the machine and add the olive oil. Process for 1 more minute and transfer the dough to a floured wooden board or a smooth work surface. Continue to knead for a couple of minutes until the dough is smooth, adding more flour if the dough is too sticky.
4. Put the pizza dough in a mixing bowl to which you have added the remaining 1 tablespoon of oil, and turn it once to coat the other side. Cover with a clean dishtowel and let the dough rise until doubled (1 1/2 to 2 hours). Punch the dough down and let it rise for 1 more hour, if possible.

HAND METHOD:

1. Combine the flour and salt, and place the mixture on a smooth work surface or in a very large bowl. Make a well in the center, and add the yeast mixture and olive oil. Gradually work the flour into the liquid, using a wooden spoon or your fingers. When the dough is too stiff to work with a spoon, knead it with your hands on a floured surface until it is smooth and shiny (about 8 to 10 minutes). Add more flour if the dough is too sticky.
2. Put the pizza dough in a mixing bowl to which you have added the remaining 1 tablespoon of oil, and turn it once to coat the other side. Cover with a clean dishtowel and let the dough rise until doubled (1 1/2 to 2 hours). Punch the dough down and let it rise for 1 more hour, if possible.

TIP   Pizza dough can be made ahead of time (even the day before) and refrigerated, covered with clear plastic wrap. It will rise in the refrigerator, but should be brought to room temperature, punched down, and, if possible, left to rise again briefly before spreading it in the pan.

Pizza Margherita

Traditional Neapolitan Pizza with Tomato Sauce, Mozzarella, and Basil

1 16-inch-diameter round pizza, 1 15- by 13-inch rectangular pizza, or 4 individual 8-inch-diameter pizzas

● When I was a college student in Florence one summer, we had an evening ritual of walking to the *Piazza San Marco* and ordering pizza at the osteria there. Each of us ordered our own individual pizza, and mine was always the simple *Margherita*: fresh tomatoes, mozzarella, and basil. And to drink, "*una Coca.*" Heaven!

Pizza Dough (page 130)
a sprinkling of cornmeal
2 cups of Tomato Sauce (facing page)
8 ounces of sliced or shredded mozzarella
a sprinkling of grated Parmesan cheese (optional)
3 to 4 leaves of fresh basil, torn
a drizzling of extra-virgin olive oil

1. Preheat the oven to 450 degrees.
2. Sprinkle a pizza pan with cornmeal and stretch the dough to fit the pan.
3. Spread the Tomato Sauce on the dough.
4. Top with the cheeses and basil.
5. Drizzle with the olive oil.
6. Bake on the lowest rack of the oven for 20 minutes, or until the crust is golden brown and the cheese is melted.

• In Italy, pizza is often topped with fresh sliced tomatoes or raw, drained canned plum tomatoes instead of a cooked tomato sauce. This recipe is for a simple cooked tomato sauce that you can use over pasta as well as for pizza.

3 tablespoons of olive oil (preferably extra-virgin)
$^1/_2$ to $^3/_4$ cup of slivered onions
1 tablespoon of garlic, finely chopped (optional)
1 28-ounce can of Italian plum tomatoes in thick purée
3 leaves of fresh basil, if available
2 teaspoons of dried oregano
salt and freshly ground pepper to taste

1. Heat the oil in a wide, shallow saucepan or skillet (9 or 10-inches in diameter, to allow the sauce to reduce quickly), and sauté the onion and garlic gently for about 2 minutes or until translucent. Add the tomatoes; crush with a fork; add the basil, oregano, salt and pepper; stir.
2. Simmer, uncovered, for 10 to 15 minutes, stirring occasionally.

Pizza con Pesto, Pomodoro, Mozzarella e Olive

•

Pesto Pizza with Plum Tomatoes, Fresh Mozzarella, and Black Olives

1 large 16-inch pizza or 4 small pizzas

• This pizza is especially colorful, with the green pesto sauce, the bright red plum tomatoes, and the black olives. I like to make these in individual sizes as a luncheon entrée with a green salad, or for a first course offering.

1 large pizza crust or 4 small pizza crusts (page 130)
1 recipe of Pesto Sauce (following page)
2 cups of ripe plum tomatoes, sliced (4 tomatoes), *or*
    2 cups of canned plum tomatoes, drained and sliced, *or*
    1 1/2 cups of sun-dried tomatoes, slivered (page 30)
2 cups of fresh mozzarella, thinly sliced or shredded
1 cup of black olives *(Gaeta* or *Kalamata)*, pitted and coarsely chopped
salt and freshly ground pepper to taste

1. Spread 1/2 cup of pesto (or more, to taste) on the raw pizza shell. For individual pizzas, use 2 or 3 tablespoons of pesto sauce on each one.
2. Arrange the tomatoes on top of the pesto. Top with the mozzarella and chopped olives. Season lightly with salt and pepper. For individual pizzas, arrange 1/4 cup of tomatoes on each pizza, then add remaining toppings.
3. For a single large pizza, bake at 450 degrees for 15 to 20 minutes, or until the crust is crispy. For individual pizzas, reduce the baking time to 10 to 15 minutes.

134

- 2 cups of fresh basil leaves (if the leaves are large, tear into pieces)
  2 tablespoons of pine nuts
  2 to 3 cloves of garlic
  salt to taste
  $1/2$ cup of grated Parmesan cheese
  3 tablespoons of grated Romano cheese
  $1/2$ to $3/4$ cup of olive oil (half olive oil and half extra-virgin)

1. Put all of the ingredients in a food processor bowl except for the olive oil. Process until the consistency is pasty, scraping the bowl occasionally.
2. Pour $1/2$ cup olive oil through the feed tube of the processor until all is evenly mixed, add the remaining $1/4$ cup oil if a more liquid consistency is desired.

CATERINA

Pizza

Quattro

Stagioni

•

*Four-
Seasons
Pizza*

8 slices

• Four Seasons Pizza derives its name from dividing the pizza into four sections, each with a different topping. There are many variations that can be substituted for those mentioned below, such as fried eggplant, anchovies, black olives, and so on.

1 recipe of Pizza Dough (page 130)
cornmeal for sprinkling on the pan
4 tablespoons of extra-virgin olive oil
1/2 cup of artichoke hearts in oil, drained well and
    sliced in half
2 tablespoons of Italian flat-leaf parsley, minced
1/2 cup of fresh mushrooms, sliced
2 cloves of garlic, minced
salt and freshly ground pepper to taste
1 cup of Tomato Sauce for Pizza (page 133)
1 whole red or green pepper, seeded and cut into strips
1 cup of mozzarella, shredded or thinly sliced
1 tablespoon of fresh basil leaves, shredded

1. Make the Pizza Dough 1 hour or more ahead of time. Let it rise in an oiled bowl.
2. Heat the oven to 450 degrees.
3. Oil a 14- to 16-inch-round pizza pan and sprinkle it with cornmeal.
4. Reserve 1/2 cup of the dough and press the remainder into the pan. Divide the reserved dough into two pieces and roll each into a 16-inch-long rope. Press onto the dough in a cross to form four quarter-sections.

5. Brush the pizza dough with 3 tablespoons of the olive oil.
6. Cover one quarter of the pizza with the artichoke hearts, and 1 tablespoon of the parsley.
7. Spread the mushrooms over the second quarter, and sprinkle with half the garlic, 1 tablespoon of the parsley, and salt and pepper to taste.
8. Cover the remaining two quarters with tomato sauce. On one quarter, place the pepper strips and $1/2$ cup of the mozzarella. On the last quarter, sprinkle the remaining mozzarella and the basil.
9. Drizzle the pizza with the remaining olive oil, and bake until the crust is golden (15 to 20 minutes).

Pizza alle Melanzane

•

Spicy Eggplant Pizza

4 8-inch pizzas

• Sicilians love eggplant. This pizza is especially spicy because of the hot pepper flakes. The addition of semolina to the all-purpose flour results in a pizza with a chewier crust.

DOUGH:

1 envelope of active dry yeast
1 teaspoon of sugar
1 cup of lukewarm water
2 1/2 cups of unbleached flour
1/2 cup of semolina flour
1 teaspoon of salt
3 tablespoons of olive oil plus additional for brushing on pizza

PIZZA TOPPING:

2 tablespoons of olive oil (preferably extra-virgin)
1 teaspoon of dried red pepper flakes (optional)
2 cups of shredded mozzarella
2 Japanese eggplants or 1 medium eggplant
3 tablespoons olive oil (or more), preferably extra-virgin
2 plum tomatoes, sliced into rounds
6 fresh basil leaves, torn
1/4 cup of freshly grated Parmesan cheese
cornmeal for sprinkling on the pizza pans

1. In a large mixing bowl, dissolve the yeast and sugar in the water. Let stand for 10 minutes or until foamy.
2. Put the unbleached flour, semolina, and salt in the bowl of a food processor and pulse for a few seconds. Add the water-yeast mixture through the feed

tube and process for 45 seconds. Add 2 tablespoons of the olive oil. Process until a smooth ball forms, adding more flour if necessary. (See page 131 for the hand method).

3. Put the dough on a floured surface and knead for 2 to 3 minutes, until smooth and elastic. Place the dough in an oiled bowl, cover with a cloth, and set in a warm place until it doubles in bulk (about 1 $^{1}/_{2}$ hours).

4. Punch down the dough and let it rest for 10 minutes. Divide the dough into four equal pieces, and roll each piece into a flat circle about 8-inches in diameter.

5. Slice Japanese eggplants lengthwise or slice medium eggplant into $^{1}/_{4}$-inch rounds. Sauté in olive oil in a nonstick pan until lightly golden. Drain on paper towels.

6. Preheat the oven to 450 degrees (see Baking Tips for Breads and Pizzas, page 128).

7. Brush each of the pizza rounds with olive oil, and sprinkle with red pepper flakes if desired. Sprinkle the mozzarella evenly over the dough circles. Top with the eggplant, tomato, and basil. Sprinkle with Parmesan cheese.

8. Place the pizzas on a baking sheet that has been dusted with cornmeal. Bake until the pizza is brown around the edges and the cheese is bubbling (about 10 to 12 minutes).

*Calzone
di
Verdura
alla
Balbina*

•

*Balbina's
Vegetable
Calzone*

6 servings

• *Calzoni* are stuffed pizzas that resemble trouser legs, or "*calzoni*" in Italian. Balbina Schiano, from the island of Ischia, gave me this recipe, which includes a filling of broccoli rabe with a bit of crushed hot pepper, minced garlic, and extra-virgin olive oil.

Another way to prepare stuffed pizza is to flatten the dough into a rectangle, spread the filling over the dough, and roll it up like a jelly roll. This is called a *stromboli*, and it is sliced in diagonal pieces and served as an appetizer. Spinach or Swiss chard are good substitutes for the broccoli rabe filling when making either *calzoni* or *stromboli*.

2 bunches of broccoli rabe
4 garlic cloves, finely minced
crushed hot pepper flakes
$^1/_4$ cup plus 2 tablespoons of extra-virgin olive oil
salt and freshly ground pepper to taste
1 recipe of Pizza Dough (page 130)
cornmeal for sprinkling on the baking sheet

1. Clean the broccoli rabe, removing all of the large, tough leaves and the lower stems. Place the florets, small leaves, and top tender stems in a colander and wash well.
2. Fill a medium stock pot halfway with salted water and bring to a boil. Add the broccoli rabe and cook, covered, for 5 to 7 minutes. Drain well in a colander.
3. Preheat the oven to 400 degrees.
4. In a 10 or 12-inch skillet, sauté the garlic, broccoli rabe, and pepper flakes in $^1/_4$ cup of olive oil for about 5 minutes, stirring to coat the broccoli rabe with

the oil. Salt and pepper to taste, remove from the heat, and cool thoroughly.

5. On a large, lightly floured board, stretch or roll out the pizza dough into a large rectangle. Spread the vegetable filling on the lower half of dough (leaving 1/2 inch uncovered at the bottom), and fold the top half over, pressing the edges down firmly with your fingers or the tines of a fork to seal in the filling.

   For individual *calzone,* divide the dough into 6 parts, press or roll them into flat oval shapes, and fill as described above. Press very well along the edges. Place the *calzoni* on a baking sheet that has been lightly brushed with olive oil and sprinkled with cornmeal.

6. Bake for 25 to 30 minutes, or until golden brown. Remove and let sit for 5 minutes before serving.

Schiacciata alle Cipolle

•

*Flatbread
with Thinly
Sliced Onions*

*10 to 12
servings*

• A tasty variation on the herbed *focaccia* (*Focaccia al Rosmarino*, page 129), this flatbread is especially dramatic if baked in a large round pizza pan. The onions give a wonderful flavor and color to the bread. Delicious served as an accompaniment to soups and salads.

Focaccia Dough (page 130)
cornmeal for sprinkling on the pan
1/4 cup of extra-virgin olive oil
1 medium onion (white or red), thinly sliced
kosher salt and freshly ground pepper

1. Let the *Focaccia* Dough rise in an oiled bowl, covered with a clean towel, for about 1 hour; punch down and let rise again. After the second rising, punch dough down again.
2. Preheat the oven to 450 degrees.
3. Stretch the dough to fit a round 16-inch pizza pan that has been sprinkled lightly with cornmeal.
4. Brush the dough with half of the olive oil and arrange the onions evenly over the crust. Sprinkle with salt and pepper, drizzle with the remaining olive oil, and let rise for another 30 minutes if possible. (If you are using a convection oven, the *Schiacciata* can be baked immediately.)
5. Bake on the lowest rack of the oven for 20 minutes, or until the *Schiacciata* is golden brown. For a crispy crust, see Baking Tips for Breads and Pizzas, page 128.

• These golden puffs of fried dough were often our Sunday-night snack before returning home to the Bronx from our grandparents' house on Long Island. All of the toppings were placed on the table with the fried dough, for us to choose as we wished.

1 recipe of Pizza Dough, risen twice (page 130)
several cups of vegetable oil or pure olive oil for
     deep frying (about 5 to 6 cups)

TOPPINGS:

2 cups of Pizza Sauce (page 133)
one small dessert cup filled with salt
one small dessert cup filled with granulated sugar
     or a shaker of confectioner's sugar

1. After punching down the dough for the second time, break off pieces the size of small oranges. Lightly stretch the dough into circles by pressing down with the palm of your hand.

2. Heat the oil to 375 degrees in a heavy, deep saucepan or electric fryer. (Test the oil by placing a small piece of decrusted bread into it; when the edges of the bread bubble and sizzle, the oil is ready.) Carefully slide the *zeppole* into the hot oil using a large, metal, pierced spoon or spatula. Do not crowd the *zeppole,* because the dough will puff up quite a bit. Turn the puffs over until they are evenly golden on both sides.

3. Remove the *zeppole,* draining off excess oil, and place them on a cookie sheet lined with paper towels. Fry the remaining dough in batches until it is all used. Transfer the puffs to a large platter and serve immediately with the toppings.

Zeppole di Grandpa Tony

•

Grandpa Tony's Fried Dough

20 puffs

Pane Origanato

•

Italian Bread Baked with Extra-Virgin Olive Oil and Oregano

6 to 10 slices, depending on the length of the loaf

• My grandfather prepared this baked bread often, especially for a meal featuring a vegetable *frittata* and a fresh tomato salad. It is fine made with a good loaf of Italian-bakery bread, and even better with a homemade loaf. Sicilian semolina bread is especially delicious prepared in this way.

1 loaf of Italian bread, preferably topped with
    sesame seeds and split in half lengthwise
1/4 cup of extra-virgin olive oil
2 teaspoons of dried oregano
a pinch of salt and a few grindings of freshly ground pepper

1. Place the bread, open, on a large cookie sheet.
2. Drizzle or brush the bread with the olive oil. Sprinkle with oregano, salt, and pepper.
3. Put the two halves together and bake at 375 degrees for 10 minutes or until the crust is crispy.
4. Slice into 2-inch sections and serve.

144

• *Panini* are the little stuffed breads or sandwiches that Italians buy at bar-cafés and eat standing up as a snack in the late morning or for lunch. They can be found at airport snack bars and in *Tavola Calda*, the Italian version of cafeterias or fast-food restaurants.

Panini can be made from hard rolls or squares of *focaccia*, sliced and filled with a variety of cured meats, such as *prosciutto* or *mortadella*, and cheese. But just as often they are filled with roasted vegetables, tomatoes and mozzarella, and all types of vegetable *frittate*.

Below are suggested fillings for vegetarian *panini*. A sprinkling of a good-quality extra-virgin olive oil will really give these tasty sandwiches an extra-special flavor.

PANINI FILLINGS:

Artichoke and pea *frittata* (*Tortino Fantasia*, page 171)
Roasted peppers with fresh mozzarella and basil
Sautéed peppers and onions with fresh basil
    (*Peperoni con Cipolla in Padella*, page 185)
Eggplant *Parmigiana* (*Melanzane alla Parmigiana*, page 158)
Roasted or grilled eggplant and zucchini with sun-dried
    tomatoes
Fresh mozzarella slices and sliced ripe tomatoes with basil
    (*Insalata Caprese*, page 31)
Zucchini, potato, and onion *frittata*
    (*Frittata di Zucchine e Cipolle*, page 170)
Goat cheese, *mascarpone*, sun-dried tomato,
    and basil spread

Sfincione

di

Grandpa

Tony

•

*Grandpa
Tony's
Sicilian Pizza*

*12 4-inch-
squares*

• This recipe is for the very traditional thick Sicilian pizza. The dough has one cup of semolina flour added to the all-purpose flour normally used for pizza. The shape is always rectangular and is cut into 4-inch squares when served. The anchovy topping with chunks of tomatoes and slivered onions is the most classic version, although when we were children we preferred a mozzarella-and-tomato topping with a sprinkling of oregano, grated Parmesan cheese, and fresh basil leaves, and a final drizzling of olive oil.

DOUGH:

1 $^1/_2$ cups of very warm water
1 package of active dry yeast
1 teaspoon of sugar
3 $^1/_4$ cups of all-purpose flour
1 cup of semolina flour
1 teaspoon of salt
1 egg, large or extra-large
2 tablespoons of olive oil plus additional for
    coating the bowl
cornmeal for sprinkling on the baking pan

TOPPING:

2 medium onions, slivered
$^1/_2$ cup of extra-virgin olive oil
1 $^1/_2$ cups of chopped plum tomatoes (fresh or canned,
    well drained)
1 tin of flat anchovy fillets, drained and halved
1 tablespoon of dried oregano (or more, to taste)
freshly ground pepper to taste
$^1/_2$ cup of dry bread crumbs

1. Combine the yeast, water, and sugar in a large measuring cup. Let sit for 5 to 10 minutes, or until foamy.
2. Put the flours and the salt into the bowl of a food processor or cake mixer. (Use the plastic dough blade or hook.)(See page 131 for the hand method.)
3. With the motor running, add the yeast-water mixture in a stream, then add the egg, and process or mix until the dough pulls away from the sides of the bowl and forms a ball. Stop the motor and add the olive oil. Process or mix again for about 1 minute. Turn the dough onto a lightly floured surface and finish kneading by hand until the dough is smooth and soft.
4. Place the dough in large mixing bowl to which you have added another tablespoonful of oil. Turn the dough to coat. Cover with a clean dishtowel and let rise in a warm place for about 1 to 1 1/2 hours, until doubled in size.
5. Punch the dough down and roll or shape it into a large rectangle to fit into your baking pan. Sprinkle the baking pan with cornmeal and place the dough into the pan, pressing the edges up against the sides.
6. Preheat the oven to 450 degrees.
7. Sauté the onions in the olive oil until translucent. Let cool slightly.
8. Place the tomatoes and onions on the dough. Top with anchovy pieces and sprinkle with oregano, pepper, and bread crumbs. Let rest, covered with a clean towel, for 30 minutes.
9. Bake for about 20 to 25 minutes, or until the crust is golden brown. (See Baking Tips for Breads and Pizzas, page 128.)

Secondi
Piatti

Pescara Market, Abruzzo

RECIPES

- *Zucchine Ripiene*
  STUFFED ZUCCHINI BOATS

- *Torta di Bietole*
  SWISS CHARD TORTE

- *Ravioli di Spinaci al Mascarpone*
  SPINACH RAVIOLI WITH TOMATO MASCARPONE CREAM SAUCE

- *Frittata di Pasta*
  SPAGHETTI PIE (OMELET)

- *Melanzane alla Parmigiana*
  EGGPLANT PARMESAN

- *Strudel di Spinaci e Ricotta*
  SPINACH-RICOTTA STRUDEL

- *Involtini di Melanzane alla Casalinga*
  EGGPLANT ROLLS CASALINGA

- *Giambotta*
  HEARTY SICILIAN VEGETABLE STEW

- *Timballo alla San Giovannella*
  ANNA TASCA LANZA'S EGGPLANT TIMBALE

- *Lasagne di Verdure alla Maria*
  MARY'S VEGETABLE LASAGNE

- *Frittata di Zucchine e Cipolle*
  OPEN-FACED ZUCCHINI AND ONION OMELET

- *Tortino Fantasia*
  BAKED FRITTATA WITH ARTICHOKE HEARTS AND TINY PEAS

- *Manicotti di Mamma*
  MOM'S MANICOTTI (CRÊPES WITH RICOTTA FILLING AND MARINARA SAUCE)

- *Peperoni Imbottiti di Chef Enrico*
  CHEF ENRICO'S STUFFED PEPPERS

*S*ECONDI PIATTI (literally, "second plates") are the main course dishes in Italian cuisine. A classical Italian menu would feature entrées of veal, fish, pork, poultry, rabbit, lamb, or—to a lesser degree—beef. The totally vegetarian diet is not as common in Italy as it is in the United States, but vegetable stews, soups, pasta, and side dishes have long been of supreme importance in the daily diet of most Italians.

I offer in this chapter some of the heartier vegetable recipes that are part of my family's favorite non-meat entrées. As with many of the recipes in this book, these will serve you well in smaller portions if used as *primi piatti*, (first courses) or *contorni* (side dishes). For example, try the *Involtini di Melanzane alla Casalinga* (Eggplant Rolls Casalinga, page 162) as *antipasti*, or the *Frittata di Zucchine e Cipolle* (Open-Faced Zucchini and Onion Omelet, page 170) as a stuffing for *panini* at lunchtime. The versatility of these substantial vegetable dishes lets you serve them in many different ways.

The use of eggs and a variety of cheeses with pasta ensures a balance of protein and carbohydrates when coupled with many fresh vegetables. Stuffed pasta dishes such as *Ravioli di Spinaci al Mascarpone* (page 156), *Cannelloni* (page 173), and layered *Lasagne di Verdure alla Maria* (page 166) are examples of this healthy combination of the daily required food groups. For more exotic fare, the *Timballo alla San Giovanella* (page 164) offers a mold of fried eggplant encasing *perciatelli* pasta combined with several cheeses and herbs in a rich marinara sauce.

Melanzane alla Parmigiana (Eggplant Parmesan, page 158), *Zucchine Ripiene* (Stuffed Zucchini Boats, page 153), *Peperoni Imbottiti di Chef Enrico* (Chef Enrico's Stuffed Peppers, page 174), and *Giambotta* (Hearty Sicilian Vegetable Stew, page 163) are recipes that highlight vegetables in their own right, with a small amount of extra-virgin olive oil and fresh herbs added to bring out marvelous flavors and textures.

It is my hope that the recipes in this main course chapter will give new importance to the vegetables you use as entrées. Many can be prepared ahead of time and even frozen, a real bonus for today's busy people. Cutting up and assembling fresh vegetables for these tasty dishes can be an enjoyable experience for the whole family. Besides, I've learned from teaching cooking to children that participation in preparing a new recipe promotes their willingness to try new fresh vegetables.

One of the most wonderful and descriptive words in the Italian language, *abbondanza* (bounty), creates for me images of the array of colorful, fresh vegetables that we harvest in the summer from my husband's garden. It is always a thrill to see, on our kitchen counters, baskets heaped with different-sized eggplants, zucchini, green and red peppers, slender and tender green beans, vibrant leafy bunches of spinach, Swiss chard, arugula, and, of course, tomatoes, tomatoes, tomatoes! If having a home garden is not possible, treat yourself to a shopping expedition to a farmer's market or a produce market known for the variety and freshness of its vegetables. Buy with the idea of trying recipes from this book that are new in your culinary experience. Create and experiment; it is difficult to fail when you are using good-quality fresh ingredients. Measurements don't have to be exact, as they do in baking recipes. Use good-quality olive oil and fresh herbs in your main course entrées, and I know your results will be fantastic. *Buona cucina*!

• Beautiful in color, this is a wonderful dish that makes use of the abundant, tender summer zucchini from your garden.

6 small zucchini, washed well
butter for greasing baking dish
$^1/_2$ cup of minced onion
3 to 4 tablespoons of olive oil (preferably extra-virgin)
2 tablespoons each of chopped flat-leaf parsley and fresh basil
3 tablespoons of grated Romano cheese
salt and freshly ground pepper to taste
4 tablespoons of canned tomato sauce or 2 plum tomatoes, chopped
1 egg, slightly beaten
3 tablespoons of grated Parmesan or cheddar cheese

1. Steam the zucchini for about 15 minutes or until tender. Cut off the ends and split the zucchini lengthwise.
2. Using a paring knife, gently scoop out the pulp leaving a thin zucchini "shell." Line up the shells in a buttered, shallow, ovenproof dish.
3. In a skillet, sauté the onion and the pulp of the zucchini in the olive oil; add the parsley and basil, the Romano cheese, and salt and pepper to taste.
4. Cook for about 15 minutes on low heat.
5. Add the chopped tomatoes or tomato sauce.
6. Transfer to a bowl, let the mixture cool slightly, then add the egg. Mix until well blended.
7. Meanwhile, preheat the oven to 350 degrees.
8. Fill the zucchini shells, and sprinkle with the Parmesan or cheddar cheese.
9. Bake for 25-30 minutes or until the cheese is melted and the boats are heated through.

Zucchine

Ripiene

•

*Stuffed
Zucchini
Boats*

*3 servings as
a main course,
6 servings as
a side dish*

• Flaky, buttery pastry and the exotic flavors of golden raisins, pine nuts, and Swiss chard make this torte a special treat. If Swiss chard is not available, fresh spinach can be substituted, although the chard has a sweeter flavor.

2 pounds of Swiss chard, washed well, tough lower stalks discarded, leaves
   and stalks cut into 3-inch pieces
4 tablespoons of extra-virgin olive oil
2 garlic cloves, finely minced
$^1/_4$ cup of sultana raisins (golden)
1 15 ounce container of ricotta cheese
3 eggs, beaten
$^2/_3$ cup of freshly grated Parmesan cheese
$^1/_4$ cup of pine nuts
salt and freshly ground pepper to taste
1 tablespoon of butter
1 sheet of frozen puff-pastry dough, thawed for 30 minutes

1 egg plus 1 tablespoon water, lightly beaten for egg wash

1. Cook the Swiss chard in 4 cups of lightly salted boiling water until tender. Drain and squeeze to remove as much water as possible. Chop coarsely.
2. In a large skillet, sauté the olive oil and garlic gently for 3 minutes. Add the Swiss chard and cook for 5 minutes to let the flavors blend. Turn off the heat and add the raisins.
3. Preheat the oven to 400 degrees.

4. Transfer the Swiss chard and raisins to a mixing bowl and stir in the ricotta, the two beaten eggs, the Parmesan, and the pine nuts. Add salt and pepper to taste.
5. Lightly grease a pie pan or 9-inch spring-form pan with butter, and roll out the pastry to line the pan, leaving 2 1/2-inch overhanging all around.
6. Fill the pastry-lined pan with the Swiss chard mixture. Fold in the pastry to cover the filling. (The center of the torte may not be totally covered with pastry, and may open somewhat during baking.)
7. Lightly beat the remaining egg with 1 tablespoon of water. Brush all exposed pastry with egg wash.
8. Bake for about 40 minutes, until puffed and golden. Remove the torte from the oven and let it rest for 10 minutes. Remove the sides of the spring-form pan, if used. Place the torte on a platter and serve it warm or at room temperature.

Ravioli di Spinaci al Mascarpone

•

Spinach Ravioli with Tomato Mascarpone Cream Sauce

4 to 5 servings as a main course

• Mascarpone is rich, and a little goes a long way. The pink of the sauce is lovely with the spinach ravioli.

1 pound of spinach ravioli, filled with ricotta or mushrooms
1 recipe of Tomato-Leek Sauce (below)
$^1/_2$ cup of *mascarpone* cheese ($^1/_2$ cup of heavy cream may be substituted)
$^3/_4$ cup of freshly grated Parmesan cheese

1. Prepare Tomato-Leek Sauce.
2. Bring 5 quarts of salted water to a boil.
3. Add the ravioli and stir periodically until they rise to the surface and are tender but not mushy. (Follow the package directions; frozen ravioli take longer.)
4. Add the *mascarpone* cheese to the Tomato-Leek Sauce and stir. Add the drained ravioli, and cook for 1 minute until the ravioli are coated with the sauce. Transfer to serving dish and pass the Parmesan.

Tomato-Leek Sauce

•

3 cups

3 tablespoons of extra-virgin olive oil
2 small leeks, the white part only, cleaned and sliced thin
1 28-ounce can of crushed tomatoes or 2 cups chopped, fresh tomatoes
salt and pepper
2 tablespoons of parsley, minced
3 to 4 leaves of fresh basil, slivered

1. In large open skillet, sauté the leeks in the olive oil until translucent.
2. Remove the pan from the flame and add the tomatoes. If using whole tomatoes, break them coarsely with a fork.
3. Add the seasonings and return to low heat, simmering for 20 minutes.

• This is a tasty dish using leftover spaghetti; your family will love it!

6 extra-large eggs
$^1/_4$ teaspoon of salt
freshly ground pepper to taste
$^1/_2$ cup of grated Parmesan cheese
3 tablespoons of fresh basil, slivered
2 tablespoons of fresh Italian flat-leaf parsley, minced
$^3/_4$ pound of leftover pasta with tomato sauce
2 tablespoons of olive oil

1. In a large bowl lightly beat the eggs with the salt and pepper, Parmesan cheese, basil, and 1 tablespoon of the parsley.
2. Stir in the pasta and mix well.
3. Heat the oil in a 12-inch non-stick frying pan with a heat-proof handle. When it is hot enough to make the eggs sizzle, add the mixture to the pan, using a fork to distribute the pasta evenly.
4. Cook over gentle heat for 12 to 15 minutes, until the *frittata* is set but not browned. Because of the density of this *frittata*, rotating the pan on the burner throughout the cooking time is essential so that all the parts are cooked evenly.
5. To finish off the top, slide the pan into the oven 6-inches under the broiler for 2 to 3 minutes, or until the surface is golden.
6. To serve, sprinkle with the remaining chopped parsley and cut into wedges. May be served warm or cold.

Frittata di Pasta

•

Spaghetti Pie (Omelet)

6 servings

Melanzane alla Parmigiana

•

Eggplant Parmesan

6 servings

• There are probably more variations of this recipe than any other eggplant dish. This version is true to my mother's recipe, although I have added a variation that I learned in Amalfi from Chef Enrico Franzese. My Sicilian friend, Mirella, omits the mozzarella and uses *Pecorino Romano* in place of the grated Parmesan cheese; she serves the eggplant immediately after frying, without baking it in the oven. In Umbria lemon zest is grated between the eggplant and cheese layers.

2 medium eggplants, sliced into $1/2$-inch rounds
2 cloves of garlic
3 to 4 tablespoons of olive oil, preferably extra-virgin
1 28-ounce can of crushed plum tomatoes or 1 $1/2$ pounds
    fresh, peeled, seeded, and chopped tomatoes
3 or 4 fresh basil leaves
salt and freshly ground pepper to taste
$1/4$ cup of flour
vegetable oil for deep frying (about 4 cups)
8 ounces of whole-milk mozzarella, sliced thin or shredded
$1/2$ to $3/4$ cup of grated Parmesan cheese
2 eggs, lightly beaten (optional, a variation from Amalfi)

1. Slice the eggplants, salt liberally, weight them down with a heavy plate, and set aside for 20 to 30 minutes.
2. While the eggplant is draining, prepare the sauce. Slice the garlic cloves in half and sauté them in olive oil over medium heat until golden (be careful not to let them burn).
3. Remove the pan from the heat and add the tomatoes, basil, salt to taste, and a few grindings of pepper, and let simmer for 15 to 20 minutes. The garlic can be discarded at this point.

4. Preheat the oven to 350 degrees.
5. Rinse the eggplant with water and squeeze dry. Pat dry with paper towels. Dredge the pieces lightly in flour, shake off the excess. In a deep fryer or sauté pan, heat 3 to 4 inches oil until a cube of bread sizzles around the edges. Fry the eggplant in hot vegetable oil until light golden on both sides. Drain well on paper towels.
6. In an oven-proof baking dish, spread a layer of the tomato sauce, then a layer of fried eggplant. Sprinkle with Parmesan cheese and a layer of the sliced or shredded mozzarella cheese. Repeat until everything is used up, finishing with the tomato sauce, a few slices of mozzarella, and a final sprinkling of Parmesan cheese. If desired, pour beaten eggs over the dish and tilt to distribute evenly before baking.
7. Bake for about 15 to 20 minutes, or until the mozzarella is melted and bubbling.

NOTE   In Amalfi and Sicily, eggplants are sliced lengthwise rather than into discs. Either method produces a delicious result!

Strudel di Spinaci e Ricotta

Spinach-
Ricotta
Strudel

4 servings

• A versatile and attractive dish, this strudel can be used as a main course or side dish, or cut into smaller slices and served as an hors d'oeuvre.

1 sheet of frozen puff-pastry dough
1 10-ounce package of chopped frozen spinach,
    thawed, drained, and well squeezed
2 tablespoons of butter
2 to 3 tablespoons of shallots, finely chopped
1 pound (or 1 15-ounce container) of whole-milk or part-skim-milk
    ricotta cheese, drained in a colander for 10 minutes
$^{1}/_{4}$ cup of Parmesan cheese, freshly grated
1 egg yolk
$^{1}/_{2}$ teaspoon of salt, or to taste
2 grindings of fresh pepper
3 grindings of fresh nutmeg
1 egg plus 1 tablespoon water for egg wash

1. Preheat the oven to 400 degrees. Line a large jellyroll pan with parchment paper.
2. Let the puff pastry thaw at room temperature for 25 to 30 minutes, or until soft enough to roll out.
3. Sauté the spinach and shallots in butter for 3 to 4 minutes, or until the liquid from the spinach is evaporated. Let it cool for 5 to 10 minutes.
4. In a large mixing bowl, combine the ricotta and Parmesan cheese; add the spinach mixture, egg yolk, and seasonings. Mix well.

160

5. With a rolling pin, roll the pastry dough on a floured board until you enlarge the rectangle to about 11 by 14 inches. Spread the filling along the length of the dough on the lower third of the rectangle. Roll up the strudel very gently, lower part first, then fold over the top, tucking in the sides, and place the strudel seam-side down on the lined jellyroll pan. Prick the top of the strudel with a fork in several places, or make 2-inch slashes down its length.
6. Lightly beat the egg with 1 tablespoon of water. Brush strudel with egg wash.
7. Bake for 35 minutes or until puffy and golden brown. Let the strudel cool slightly before cutting it into diagonal slices.

To decorate the strudel for festive occasions, roll out one third of another sheet of puff pastry to about 1/4-inch thickness. Use small cookie cutters such as stars, bells, or flowers. Cut out the desired shapes and paint them with egg wash (1 egg lightly beaten with 1 tablespoon of water). Use more egg wash to glue the shapes along the length of the strudel. Paint the rest of the strudel with egg wash and bake.

Involtini di

Melanzane

alla

Casalinga

•

Eggplant Rolls
Casalinga

6 to 8 servings

• These delicious stuffed eggplant rolls can be used as a main course. My mother served them as a side dish, and the Charleston Ristorante in Mondello, Sicily featured them as part of an *antipasto* buffet.

2 medium eggplants
flour for dredging
vegetable oil for deep frying (about 4 to 6 cups)
1 pound of ricotta
1 tablespoon of flat-leaf Italian parsley, finely chopped
$^{1}/_{4}$ cup of grated Parmesan cheese
$^{1}/_{2}$ pound of mozzarella, cut into $^{1}/_{4}$-inch-thick fingers
2 cups of Marinara sauce (page 88)
salt and freshly ground pepper to taste
fresh basil leaves, if desired

1. Remove both ends and slice the eggplants lengthwise, about $^{1}/_{4}$-inch thick. Salt and let them stand for $^{1}/_{2}$ hour in a collander with a heavy plate or pan as a weight on top.
2. Rinse the eggplant slices and pat them dry with paper towels. Dredge lightly in flour. In a deep skillet with at least 2 inches of oil, deep-fry the slices until light golden. Drain on paper towels.
3. Preheat the oven to 350 degrees.
4. Mix the ricotta, 1 tablespoon of the parsley, the Parmesan, and the salt and pepper. Place a scoop (approximately 1 heaping tablespoon) of this mixture in the middle of each eggplant slice. Top with a finger of mozzarella, and then roll the eggplant from the narrow end up.
5. Place the eggplant rolls in an oiled shallow baking dish, seam-side down, and top with Marinara Sauce.
6. Bake for 20 to 25 minutes. Garnish with chopped parsley or fresh basil leaves if desired. Serve hot.

● This hearty vegetable stew is fabulous in any season. Wonderful in the cold of winter, it is especially good with crusty Italian bread or a freshly baked *focaccia*. In the summer, when the peppers are fresh out of the garden, chunks of zucchini and Japanese eggplant can be added and the potatoes omitted.

1 1/2 pounds of mixed red and green peppers,
    (yellow and orange may be used as well),
     cleaned, seeded, and sliced into thin strips
2 onions, slivered
3 baking potatoes, peeled and sliced thin (optional)
6 fresh, ripe plum tomatoes, seeded and chopped,
    or 2 cups of canned crushed tomatoes
salt and freshly ground pepper to taste
4 fresh basil leaves, torn
1/3 cup of extra-virgin olive oil

1. Preheat the oven to 350 degrees.
2. In a large baking pan, arrange the peppers, onions, potatoes, and tomatoes, and season with salt, pepper, and basil.
3. Drizzle olive oil over the mixture and place the pan in the oven for 45 minutes to an hour, or until the potatoes are tender. While baking, stir several times to avoid letting the top of the vegetables brown too much.

TIP   The casserole can be covered during the first half of the cooking time to soften the vegetables, then uncovered for the remaining time. Remember to stir after uncovering the dish.

Giambotta

●

*Hearty Sicilian
Vegetable Stew*

4 to 6 servings

Timballo alla San Giovannella

•

Anna Tasca Lanza's Eggplant Timbale

8 servings

• All of us who journeyed to Anna Tasca Lanza's Cooking School at Regaleali, Sicily were treated to this stunning, delicious eggplant-pasta molded dish, called a *timballo* or *sformato* in Italian. This recipe is adapted from Anna's cookbook, *The Flavors of Sicily* (Clarkson-Potter, 1996).

3 large eggplants (about 2 1/4 pounds)
salt
3 tablespoons of unsalted butter
1/2 cup of dry bread crumbs
vegetable oil, for deep frying
1 pound of *perciatelli* (or *bucatini*)
3 cups of thick tomato sauce, preferably homemade (page 88)
1 tablespoon of dried oregano
3 tablespoons of fresh basil, chopped or 1 teaspoon of dried basil
1 cup of mixed grated Parmesan, *Caciocavallo,* and *Pecorino*
salt and freshly ground pepper or hot crushed red pepper to taste

1. At least 1 1/2 hours before serving, peel the eggplants and slice them lengthwise 3/8 -inch thick. Salt them and let them stand in a colander for 30 minutes.
2. Meanwhile, use 1 tablespoon of the butter to lightly coat a 10-inch mold with 3-inch sides or a 10-inch springform pan. Coat evenly with 2 table-spoons of the bread crumbs.
3. Blot the eggplant slices dry. In a large skillet over medium-high heat, deep-fry the slices in the oil until lightly golden on both sides. Drain on paper towels. Set some slices aside for the top of the *timbale*. Line the bottom of the mold or pan with the reserved slices of eggplant, making an attractive arrangement (when the *timbale* is unmolded, the bottom will be the top). Line the sides with the rest of the slices, slightly over-lapping them and let-ting them hang over the edge of the pan. If you have any slices left over, set them aside to make a layer in the middle. Set mold aside.

4. Preheat the oven to 350 degrees.
5. Cook the *perciatelli* in boiling salted water for 3 minutes or until less than *al dente*, since it will cook further in the oven. Drain and return to the pot.
6. Warm the tomato sauce if cold. Stir 2 cups of the sauce and the oregano, basil, and cheese into the pasta. Add salt and pepper or hot pepper to taste. Spoon half into the lined mold. Cover with a layer of eggplant if you have slices left over, and add the rest of the *perciatelli*. Lightly press down with your hands to spread the pasta mixture to the sides. Fold the over-hanging slices of eggplant over the pasta, and cover completely with the reserved slices.
7. Sprinkle the top with the remaining bread crumbs, and dot with the remaining 2 tablespoons of butter. Bake for 25 minutes, or until golden brown on top.
8. Remove from the oven. Let stand for at least 10 minutes before unmolding. To unmold, put a platter on top and invert the pan. Remove the sides and bottom of the pan. Serve with the remaining tomato sauce on the side.

NOTE   If you prefer, brush the eggplant slices with oil and broil them until lightly browned. Grease the pan generously with butter. The dish will be less oily.

Lasagne

di

Verdure

alla

Maria

•

Mary's Vegetable Lasagne

8 generous servings

• Mary Kimberlin and I have been sharing our love of Italian cooking for 15 years. Her vegetable lasagne is light, delicious, and low in fat, and it can be prepared ahead of time. It also freezes well after baking and cooling. Béchamel sauce is optional; it gives a slightly richer flavor to the lasagne.

TOMATO SAUCE (CAN BE PREPARED AHEAD):

2 28-ounce cans of recipe-ready crushed tomatoes
1 15-ounce can of stewed tomatoes (Del Monte, Original Recipe)
1 $1/3$ cups of carrots (about $1/2$-inch in diameter), sliced $1/8$-inch thick
1 medium onion, chopped
1 small green pepper, diced
$1/2$ pound of fresh mushrooms, sliced $1/8$-inch thick
6 leaves of fresh basil, shredded into small pieces
$3/4$ teaspoon of fennel seed (optional)
2 to 3 tablespoons of olive oil
1 pound of zucchini (about 1 inch in diameter), ends removed,
    sliced $1/8$-inch thick with skin intact
salt and freshly ground pepper to taste

1. Pour the crushed tomatoes into a large stainless steel or enamel saucepan. Add the stewed tomatoes, and bring the sauce to a boil.
2. Add the carrots, onion, green pepper, mushrooms, and basil, and simmer so that the sauce bubbles gently for 25 minutes, uncovered. Stir occasionally. Add the fennel seed if desired.
3. Meanwhile, heat the olive oil in a heavy saucepan over medium heat. When the oil is hot, sauté the zucchini until lightly browned.

4. Add the sautéed zucchini to the sauce and continue cooking, uncovered, for 25 to 30 minutes more, or until the vegetables are tender but not too soft. Add salt and pepper to taste.

SPINACH CHEESE FILLING (CAN BE PREPARED 1 DAY AHEAD):

1 tablespoon of unsalted butter
1 10-ounce package of frozen chopped spinach,
    thawed and squeezed completely dry
1 15-ounce container of ricotta cheese (part skim)
$^{1}/_{2}$ pound of mozzarella cheese (part skim), grated
$^{1}/_{2}$ cup of Parmesan cheese, finely grated
1 large egg, beaten slightly
2 tablespoons of fresh parsley, finely minced
salt and freshly ground pepper to taste
a few grindings of fresh nutmeg

1 package lasagna noodles or 1 pound fresh pasta sheets
    or 1 package no-cook lasagna noodles
1 recipe Béchamel Sauce (page 169)
1 tablespoon butter

1. Melt the butter in a heavy, non-stick skillet over medium heat. Add the spinach and cook until moisture evaporates (approximately 5 to 6 minutes), being careful not to brown. Remove from the heat and cool.
2. Mix the rest of the filling ingredients together in a bowl. Add the spinach and mix well. The filling will be dry. Cover the filling and refrigerate it while sauce finishes cooking.

3. Cook pasta according to directions, or use a no-boil type. If you are cooking the pasta, use 5 to 6 quarts of salted water per pound. Do not add oil to the cooking water; it decreases the pasta's ability to absorb sauce. Cook only to the *al dente* stage (firm but tender). If using no-boil pasta, soak the sheets of pasta in warm water until they become soft and pliable (about 5 minutes). For either type, dry the pasta sheets well on paper towels before assembling the lasagne.

4. Put a thin film of the Tomato Sauce mixture on the bottom of a 9 by 13-inch baking dish. Place a layer of pasta sheets over it. If using the no-boil type, place the sheets side by side; *do not overlap them.*

5. Spread half the Spinach Cheese Filling evenly over the pasta. Pour some of the tomato sauce mixture over the Spinach Cheese Filling, making sure all of the filling is covered. Repeat layering as above, finishing with a layer of pasta covered with Tomato Sauce. Sprinkle the lasagne with Parmesan cheese.

IF YOU WILL BE SERVING THE LASAGNE IMMEDIATELY AFTER COOKING:

1. Preheat the oven to 375 degrees.
2. Make Béchamel Sauce. Pour it over the Tomato Sauce, covering it completely.
3. Sprinkle grated Parmesan cheese over the Béchamel Sauce. Dot evenly with 1 tablespoon of butter, cut into small pieces.
4. Bake for 20 minutes, or until the sauce bubbles throughout the layers. Allow the lasagne to settle before serving.

IF YOU ARE PLANNING TO SERVE THE LASAGNE AT A LATER DATE:

1. Refrigerate or freeze the assembled dish without Béchamel Sauce.
2. When you are ready to serve the lasagne, make the Béchamel Sauce and pour it over the defrosted lasagne before baking.

- 2 tablespoons of unsalted butter
  2 tablespoons of unbleached, all-purpose flour
  2 $^1/_2$ cups of whole milk
  a few grindings of white pepper
  freshly grated nutmeg

1. Melt the butter in a heavy stainless steel saucepan over medium-low heat.
2. Add the flour and stir constantly for 2 to 3 minutes, cooking roux so that it bubbles gently and does not brown.
3. Add all of the milk at once, stirring continuously with a whisk.
4. Increase the heat to medium, and stir the sauce almost continuously for about 15 to 20 minutes, until it thickens. Do not allow the sauce to stick to the bottom of the pan and burn.
5. Remove the sauce from the heat. Season with the white pepper and nutmeg. The sauce does become thicker as it cools, and can be thinned by adding more milk. For a reduced fat/cholesterol sauce, use 2-percent milk.

Frittata di Zucchine e Cipolle

•

Open-Faced Zucchini and Onion Omelet

4 to 6 servings

• Vegetable omelets, or *frittate,* are the most versatile of dishes. They can be used as main luncheon or light supper entrées with a side salad of fresh tomatoes and basil (page 31) and a crusty loaf of Italian bread (*Pane Origanato,* page 144), or use as a filling for *panini* (page 145). For a heartier dish add a sliced potato, sautéed along with the zucchini. Great for brunches and picnics, I have always enjoyed making *frittate* for my family and friends.

1 medium yellow onion, slivered
3 to 4 tablespoons of extra-virgin olive oil
2 medium or 4 small zucchini, ends removed, sliced into $^1/_4$-inch discs
3 tablespoons of butter
salt and freshly ground pepper to taste
6 extra large eggs, well beaten
$^2/_3$ cup of freshly grated Parmesan cheese
4 fresh basil leaves, torn
2 tablespoons of fresh flat-leaf Italian parsley, finely minced

1. Preheat the oven to 350 degrees.
2. In a large 10 or 12-inch skillet with an oven-proof handle, cook the onion in the olive oil over moderate heat until translucent (about 3 to 4 minutes).
3. Add the butter and the sliced zucchini and cook over medium heat, turning until the zucchini are lightly browned on both sides. Salt and pepper to taste.
4. In a medium bowl, beat the eggs, add the Parmesan, basil, and parsley, and mix well. Pour over the zucchini, rotating the skillet until the ingredients of the *frittata* are evenly distributed. Cook over moderate heat until the bottom sets (about 5 more minutes).
5. Transfer the *frittata* to the oven and bake until the top is golden brown (about 15 to 20 minutes).
6. Turn the *frittata* onto a large round serving platter and slice into wedges. Serve hot or at room temperature.

• When fresh baby artichokes are available, this *frittata* is even more delicious! Another suggestion is to make *Tortino* with asparagus and shallots.

2 tablespoons of olive oil
1 tablespoon of butter
1/2 package of frozen artichoke hearts, thawed and halved
1 garlic clove, minced
1/2 of a 10-ounce package of frozen peas, thawed
salt and freshly ground pepper to taste
2 tablespoons of fresh parsley, minced
6 extra-large eggs, well beaten
1/4 cup of Parmesan cheese, freshly grated
2 tablespoons of milk

1. Preheat the oven to 350 degrees.
2. In a 12-inch heavy stainless or other ovenproof skillet, warm the oil and butter over moderate heat. Add the artichokes and garlic and cook for 5 minutes, shaking the pan to prevent sticking. Add the peas, and cook for 5 more minutes. Season to taste with salt and pepper. Add the parsley, stir, cover, and reduce the heat to low.
3. In a medium bowl, mix the eggs, Parmesan, and milk.
4. Pour over the vegetables, rotating the skillet until the ingredients of the frittata are evenly distributed. Cook over moderate heat until the bottom sets (about 5 more minutes).
5. Place the skillet in the oven and bake until the top is golden brown (about 15 to 20 minutes).
6. Turn the *tortino* onto a large round serving dish if you wish, and slice.

Tortino Fantasia

•

Baked Frittata with Artichoke Hearts and Tiny Peas

4 to 6 servings

Manicotti

di

Mamma

•

*Mom's
Manicotti
(Crêpes with
Ricotta Filling
and Marinara
Sauce)*

*12 to 15
crêpes*

• In Italy, filled crêpes are called *crespelle*. In our family, we called my mother's fluffy ricotta-stuffed crêpes, "manicotti." I offer, in this recipe, the traditional filling she made most often, as well as the version for *cannelloni*, with the addition of spinach and *besciamella* (white sauce) as a final topping before baking.

1 cup of flour
3 eggs
a pinch of salt
2 tablespoons of butter (softened)
oil or butter to season the crêpe pan
1 recipe of basic Marinara Sauce (page 88)

FILLING (MAY BE MADE AHEAD AND REFRIGERATED):

1 1/2 pounds of ricotta cheese
1/4 cup of Parmesan cheese, freshly grated
1 large egg yolk
2 tablespoons of flat-leaf Italian parsley, finely minced
freshly ground pepper
8 ounces of mozzarella, sliced into thin finger-shapes
    (about 3-inches long)

1. In a food processor or blender, blend 1 cup of water with the flour, eggs, salt, and butter for 5 seconds. Turn off the motor and, with a rubber spatula, scrape down the sides of the container. Blend the batter for 20 seconds more, transfer it to a bowl, and let it stand, covered with plastic wrap, for 1 hour.

2. Season a crêpe pan with a little oil or butter, and heat it over high heat. Pour in just enough batter to cover the bottom of the pan. Pour off excess batter. When lightly brown on the underside, turn the crêpe over and cook it for

another 1 or 2 minutes. Slide onto a sheet of waxed paper. Repeat until all of the batter is used.

3. Preheat the oven to 350 degrees.
4. Prepare the filling by mixing all the ingredients together in a bowl.
5. Spread a dollop of filling across the center of each crêpe, place a mozzarella "finger" on top, and fold the crêpe up, tucking in the sides as you go along.
6. Ladle a few spoonfuls of Marinara Sauce on the bottom of a baking dish and lay the filled crêpes in the dish side by side, with the seam side down, leaving ample room between them for expansion. Spoon additional Marinara Sauce over the top of the manicotti.
7. Bake for 20 to 25 minutes.

TIP   The crêpes may be made and filled ahead of time and frozen, well wrapped in plastic wrap and foil. When you are ready to serve them, bake as in Steps 6 and 7. It may require slightly longer cooking time if the crêpes are frozen.

FILLING VARIATION FOR CANNELLONI:

Add 1 10-ounce package of frozen chopped spinach, thawed and squeezed dry, to the ricotta filling. Omit the parsley and mozzarella. Top with Béchamel sauce (page 169) and dot with 4 tablespoons of butter before baking.

Peperoni Imbottiti di Chef Enrico

Chef Enrico's Stuffed Peppers

4 servings

• This dish always reminds me of Amalfi, the land of capers, tomatoes, and olives, and the Luna Convento Cooking School.

4 whole green, red, and/or yellow bell peppers
9 slices of bread, decrusted and cubed
6 tablespoons of extra-virgin olive oil (or more, to taste)
1 small eggplant, cut in small dice
2/3 cup of black olives, pitted and chopped (*Gaeta* or *Kalamata*)
3 tablespoons of capers, rinsed
4 anchovy fillets, mashed with a fork (optional)
2 cloves of garlic, finely chopped
2 tablespoons of parsley, finely chopped
1 teaspoon of oregano, or to taste
2 plum tomatoes, seeded and chopped or 1/2 cup of canned crushed tomatoes
salt and freshly ground pepper to taste
1/4 cup of freshly grated Parmesan or Romano cheese
1 whole onion, thinly sliced

1. Preheat the oven to 400 degrees.
2. Slice the tops off the peppers and remove the seeds, reserving the tops.
3. Sauté the bread cubes in 1 tablespoon of the olive oil until golden crisp.
4. In a large bowl, mix together the bread cubes, 3 tablespoons (or more) of the olive oil and all the remaining ingredients except the onion, salt, and pepper. Stuff the peppers, closing with the tops.
5. Place the onions on the bottom of an ovenproof dish. Place the stuffed peppers on top, pour over 2 tablespoons or more of the olive oil, and season with salt and pepper to taste.
6. Bake for 1 hour, adding water if necessary.

Contorni

RECIPES

- ### Polenta alla Pizzaiola
  CORNMEAL SQUARES WITH SPICY TOMATO SAUCE

- ### Gattò di Patate
  PARMESAN MASHED POTATO PIE

- ### Fagiolini Aglio e Olio con Prezzemolo
  GREEN BEANS WITH GARLIC AND PARSLEY

- ### Peperoni con Cipolle in Padella
  FRIED PEPPERS AND ONIONS

- ### Bietole in Padella
  SWISS CHARD SAUTÉED IN GARLIC AND OIL

- ### Funghi al Forno
  MUSHROOMS BAKED IN THE OVEN

- ### Zucchine al Forno di Nana
  NANA'S OVEN-BAKED ZUCCHINI STICKS

- ### Patate Origanate
  OVEN-BAKED POTATO SLICES WITH OREGANO

- ### Carciofi Imbottiti alla Siciliana
  STUFFED ARTICHOKES SICILIAN STYLE

- ### Asparagi alla Parmigiana
  ASPARAGUS BAKED WITH PARMESAN CHEESE

*T*HE WORD *CONTORNI* signifies side dishes on an Italian menu. The versatility of these vegetable side dishes is one of the outstanding characteristics of Italian cuisine. Each of the *contorni* offered in this chapter could stand on its own merits as a starter course (*antipasto*) or, in some cases, as a main course (*secondo piatto*). It is not unusual in our home to serve more than one vegetable side dish with a meal.

In Italy, the *contorni* will vary with the season of the year; you will see an abundance of artichokes, fava beans, and asparagus in the spring. Spinach, arugula, and Swiss chard arrive in early summer, followed by zucchini, green beans, peppers, and tomatoes, then eggplants, cauliflower, and broccoli into the late fall. Markets abound with mushrooms, in particular porcini during this season.

Italians are so passionate about using vegetables freshly picked from their own gardens or purchased daily at the local markets, that the preparation of these earthly treasures is usually very simple. The marriage of a few tablespoons of extra-virgin olive oil and garlic, sautéed together before the addition of tender *fagiolini* (green beans), produces a sublime result. Similar treatment of fresh spinach or Swiss chard takes on an exotic twist with a simple sprinkling of *pinoli* nuts and sultana raisins.

My husband and I made a trip to the Amalfi coast to celebrate our twenty-fifth wedding anniversary. A favorite memory from that trip was our daily lunch at the *stuccheria* (snack bar) perched on a cliff hundreds of meters above the sea and a short walk from our elegant hotel. The *stuccheria* was owned by a family of three: mother, father, and 13-year-old daughter, who helped serve the customers. The *signora* would ask us what we desired from her garden that day. We gave our order, which almost always included vine-ripened tomatoes, *mozzarella di bufala*—so famous in the region of *Campania*—and, of course, just-picked basil. She then would disappear into her house adjacent to the snack bar. There, she prepared a plate of fried zucchini or eggplant which she had snatched from the vine on her way into the kitchen. We were in paradise! The quest for the freshest possible vegetables is so great that some of the restaurateurs raise their own produce and grow their own olives for the extra-virgin olive oil used in their dishes.

This chapter begins with *polenta*, the coarse-grained cornmeal so popular in northern Italy and served in a variety of dishes from *antipasti* to desserts. Very simple recipes follow for spinach, green beans, broccoli, Swiss chard, fried peppers and onions, asparagus, zucchini, potatoes, and mushrooms. Finally, the rich and delicious Sicilian stuffed artichokes complete just a sampling of the wealth of simple but intriguing treatments of *verdure* as *contorni* in Italian cuisine.

• *Polenta* is a variety of cornmeal mush or porridge very popular in the north of Italy. Because it is so often used in combination with rich vegetable sauces, I have included it in the *contorni* chapter of the book. You would be very likely to find it, however, listed as a *primi* (first course) on an Italian menu, since it can be eaten "soft" with a sauce, in place of a pasta or *risotto* dish. Grilling squares of solidified *polenta* and topping them with assorted vegetables or relishes, such as *Caponata* (page 32) or a mushroom-olive spread, allows you to use polenta as *crostini* and serve them as *antipasti*. As a main course, *polenta* can be a *sformato*—a molded dish—served with a rich ragù of vegetables.

Finally, *polenta* is sometimes an ingredient in *dolci* (dessert) recipes. There are cakes and tortes which use this dish made of coarse-grained cornmeal in place of flour. I buy imported Italian coarse-grained cornmeal since the results are often better than using domestic cornmeal, which can be too fine. Most markets, organic grocery stores, and Italian specialty markets carry *polenta*. The recipe below is prepared in the traditional way.

POLENTA:

1 tablespoon of salt
2 cups of coarse-grained Italian cornmeal
7 cups water
oil for brushing on the baking pan

1. In a large, deep, heavy saucepan, bring 7 cups of water and the salt to a boil.
2. Add the cornmeal in a steady stream (I use a large measuring cup with a spout), while stirring constantly with a long wooden spoon. The constant stirring prevents lumps from forming. After 25 to 30 minutes, the *polenta* should be thick and can easily be pulled away from the side of the pan.

Polenta alla Pizzaiola

•

Cornmeal Squares with Spicy Tomato Sauce

8 servings

3. Mound the soft polenta in a bowl or on a plate if you wish to serve it "loose." Alternatively, spread the polenta evenly on a long, flat, jelly-roll pan that has been coated with oil (I use olive oil, but you may use vegetable or corn oil if you wish). Let it stand for at least 15 to 20 minutes, or until firm.
4. Cut the polenta into squares of any desired size, and grill, fry, or bake them until heated through. Serve with Pizzaiola Sauce (below) or *Salsa alle Verdure* (page 104).

TIP   An alternative to Step 2 is to cook the mixture of salt, water, and corn-meal in a covered bowl in a microwave oven, on high power, stirring several times until creamy (about 24 minutes).

PIZZAIOLA SAUCE:

1 medium onion, cut into slivers
2 cloves of garlic, minced
3 tablespoons of extra-virgin olive oil
1 28-ounce can of plum tomatoes or 1 can
    of recipe-ready crushed tomatoes
a pinch of crushed red pepper flakes (optional)
salt and freshly ground pepper to taste
2 teaspoons of dry oregano
3 fresh basil leaves, torn

1. In a large open skillet, sauté the onion and garlic in the olive oil until translucent (about 3 minutes).
2. Pour in the tomatoes. If using whole plum tomatoes, crush them with a fork, but leave them in chunks.

3. Add the seasonings and herbs and let the mixture simmer on low heat for 20 to 25 minutes.
4. Place the warm polenta squares on a platter and top with some of the sauce. Pass the rest of the sauce separately.

VARIATION   Porcini mushrooms are particularly good with *polenta*. As a variation, soak 1 ounce of dried porcinis in 1 cup of warm water for 20 minutes. Make the Pizzaiola Sauce, but substitute 1 tablespoon of minced parsley for the oregano. Drain the mushrooms, strain the liquid and reserve. Coarsely chop the mushrooms and add them to the sauce along with $1/2$ cup of the soaking liquid. Cook the mushrooms in the sauce for an additional 10 minutes.

Gattò di Patate

•

Parmesan Mashed Potato Pie

6 to 8 servings

• In Amalfi, this dish is made with cubed mozzarella and hard-boiled egg, as well as diced salami. I use this meatless version as part of our Italian-American Thanksgiving Feast. It can be made ahead of time and refrigerated. The Parmesan cheese, parsley, and nutmeg add a real sparkle to standard mashed potato recipes.

6 Idaho baking potatoes, 8 ounces each, peeled and quartered
4 tablespoons ($^{1}/_{2}$ stick) of unsalted butter, at room temperature
       plus 2 tablespoons of butter or margarine
$^{2}/_{3}$ cup of milk, heated
$^{1}/_{3}$ cup of sour cream
$^{1}/_{2}$ cup of freshly grated Parmesan cheese
a pinch of ground nutmeg
salt and freshly ground pepper to taste
2 tablespoons of Italian flat-leaf parsley, minced (optional)
$^{1}/_{3}$ cup of fine bread crumbs
a sprinkling of paprika

1. Preheat the oven to 350 degrees.
2. Place the potatoes in a saucepan, cover with cold water, and bring to a boil. Reduce the heat slightly and cook until the potatoes are tender (20 to 30 minutes). Drain the potatoes, return them to the saucepan, and shake the pan over low heat to remove the remaining moisture (10 to 15 seconds).
3. Transfer the potatoes to a mixing bowl or to the bowl of an electric mixer.

Begin mashing with the electric mixer or by hand, and add the butter, hot milk, sour cream, Parmesan cheese, nutmeg, salt, pepper, and parsley. Continue beating until smooth; make sure there are no lumps.

4. Grease a 9-inch oven-proof pie dish with 2 tablespoons of butter or margarine. Spread the mashed potatoes evenly in the dish. Sprinkle with the bread crumbs and paprika.

5. Bake for 20 minutes or until the top is brown. Cut into wedges and serve.

TIP   This recipe can be made ahead and refrigerated until baking time.

Fagiolini Aglio e Olio con Prezzemolo

•

Green Beans with Garlic and Parsley

6 servings

• Our family often eats string beans this way. In the summer, when fresh plum tomatoes are so abundant, they can be diced and added to the beans for the last 3 to 4 minutes of cooking.

1 1/2 pounds of whole string beans, with tips removed,
    cut in half
3 tablespoons of extra-virgin olive oil
3 whole cloves of garlic
2 tablespoons of Italian flat-leaf parsley, minced
3 fresh basil leaves, torn
salt and freshly ground pepper to taste

1. Bring 2 cups of salted water to a boil in a medium saucepan.
2. Add the beans, and cook just until crisp-tender (about 8 minutes).
3. Drain the beans and set them aside.
4. In the same saucepan, sauté the garlic cloves in the olive oil until translucent, not brown.
5. Add the beans, toss to coat with oil, add herbs, salt, and pepper to taste, and cook on low heat for about 3 to 4 minutes. Remove the garlic cloves before serving. Serve hot or at room temperature.

● This simple, colorful dish was a staple in our Sicilian cooking. Sometimes we put the onion-pepper mixture into a crusty hard roll or a wedge of Italian bread and ate it as a *panini* (sandwich). Other times, we mixed the peppers and onions with lightly beaten eggs and fresh minced parsley, fried them, and made a hearty pepper-and-egg hero. Both ways it was simply delicious!

4 large bell peppers (red, yellow, and green mixed, if possible),
    cored, seeded, and cut into strips
1 large sweet yellow onion, slivered
$^1/_4$ cup of extra-virgin olive oil, or more to taste
salt and freshly ground pepper to taste

In a large skillet or wok, sauté the pepper strips and onion in the olive oil over medium heat until golden (about 10 to 15 minutes). Season with salt and pepper. Serve hot or at room temperature.

TIP   A sprinkling of pitted, chopped black olives and capers adds a spicy Neapolitan touch to this dish.

Deperoni con Cipolle in Padella

●

Fried Peppers and Onions

5 to 6 servings as a side dish

• The simplicity of preparation results in such a tasty vegetable dish that you will want to make it often when the chard is in season. We grow it in our garden from late June until the heavy frost in November. Try this recipe with the same quantity of fresh spinach. I have also seen heaping platters of sautéed spinach on *antipasti* buffets in the restaurants of Italy.

Swiss Chard Sautéed in Garlic and Oil

4 to 5 servings as a side dish

3 tablespoons of extra-virgin olive oil
3 cloves garlic, peeled, left whole
1 1/2 pounds of fresh Swiss chard, washed well,
    stems and leaves cut into 3-inch lengths
salt and freshly ground pepper to taste

1. In a large skillet or wok, sauté the garlic in the olive oil until translucent, not brown. Add the chard with water still clinging to its leaves and stalks. Cover, lower the heat, and cook for several minutes until the chard wilts. (Cooking time will depend on how young and tender the Swiss chard is.)
2. Uncover, stir well, season with salt and pepper, remove the garlic cloves, and serve.

• Maria Lo Pinto included this recipe in her book, *The Art of Italian Cooking*, published in 1948. I have been preparing this dish since I was a bride, 30 years ago.

2 1/2 pounds mushrooms, wiped clean, large mushrooms halved
3 tablespoons of parsley, chopped
3 cloves of garlic, chopped
1/2 teaspoon of oregano
1 cup of bread crumbs
5 tablespoons of grated Parmesan cheese
1/3 cup of olive oil, preferably extra-virgin
salt and freshly ground pepper to taste

1. Preheat the oven to 350 degrees.
2. Place the mushrooms in a baking dish that has been brushed with olive oil.
3. Sprinkle with the parsley, garlic, oregano, half of the bread crumbs, and the cheese. Add salt and pepper to taste.
4. Pour the rest of the oil over the mushrooms and herbs. Sprinkle with the remaining bread crumbs.
5. Bake for about 25 minutes, or until the mushrooms are tender and golden.
6. If the mushrooms become too dry, add 1/3 cup of hot water and bake 5 minutes longer. Serve very hot.

Funghi al Forno

•

Mushrooms Baked in the Oven

8 to 10 servings

Zucchine

al Forno

di Nana

•

*Nana's Oven-
Baked
Zucchini
Sticks*

*6 to 8
servings*

• These zucchini sticks are so popular with my children that I've often taught this recipe in my "Kids Cook Italian" series.

3 medium-large zucchini, ends removed, skin intact
$^1/_2$ cup of olive oil or melted butter
1 $^1/_2$ cups of bread crumbs
salt and freshly ground pepper to taste
fresh basil and parsley or $^1/_2$ teaspoon each of dried oregano and marjoram
$^1/_2$ cup of grated Parmesan cheese (optional, may be added to the crumb
    mixture)

1. Cut the zucchini in half lengthwise. Then cut each half once across the middle. Divide the quarters into sticks about $^1/_2$-inch thick.
2. Mix the bread crumbs with the seasonings and herbs (and the Parmesan, if desired) on a sheet of waxed paper.
3. Preheat the oven to 375 degrees.
4. Melt the butter or put the olive oil in an 8-inch pie pan.
5. Dip the zucchini sticks in the oil or butter, and then roll them in the bread crumb mixture.
6. Place on an ungreased cookie sheet and bake for 20 minutes or until crispy.

ALTERNATIVE METHOD:

Pour the butter or olive oil into a large bowl, add the zucchini sticks, and toss by hand until all of the sticks are coated. Proceed with the breading step.

• I think of these wonderful herbed potato slices as Italian potato chips. They are so easy to prepare, but be careful: they disappear quickly, so you may want to make extra!

8 large baking potatoes, well scrubbed, with skins left intact
$^{1}/_{4}$ cup of olive oil, or more to taste
1 $^{1}/_{2}$ tablespoons of dry oregano
salt and freshly ground pepper to taste

1. Brush a very large flat baking sheet liberally with olive oil.
2. Preheat the oven to 400 degrees. (Convection ovens are great for this recipe.)
3. Slice the potatoes $^{1}/_{4}$-inch thick (you can use the slicing disc of a food processor). Place the potato slices on the baking sheet in rows, turning each slice to coat it with oil. (You may need a second baking pan.)
4. Sprinkle with oregano, salt, and pepper.
5. Bake for 25 to 30 minutes, or until crisp and golden brown.

Patate

Origanate

•

*Oven-Baked
Potato Slices
with Oregano*

6 to 8 servings

Carciofi Imbottiti alla Siciliana

•

Stuffed Artichokes Sicilian Style

4 servings

• Aunt Marie and Aunt Jo always served stuffed artichokes on their Sunday dinner menu. Artichokes made this way are delicious and filling. The anticipation of reaching the tender heart (after all of the stuffed leaves are eaten) is the best part!

4 large artichokes
a bowl of cold water
2 tablespoons of lemon juice
1 $^{1}/_{4}$ cups of toasted breadcrumbs
$^{1}/_{4}$ cup of grated Romano cheese
$^{1}/_{4}$ cup of parsley, finely minced
2 cloves of garlic, finely chopped
salt and freshly ground pepper to taste
4 tablespoons of olive oil, preferably extra-virgin (or more to taste)

1. With a serrated knife, cut the stem off each artichoke at its base. Cut across the top of each artichoke to a depth of about 1 inch, and remove all the tough outer leaves. Using kitchen scissors, snip off the tips of the remaining leaves and wash the artichokes carefully. Put the lemon juice in the bowl of water, and soak the artichokes in the water for 5 minutes. Drain, shaking out all the water from each artichoke, and tap them on the counter to spread the leaves open.

2. Mix the bread crumbs, cheese, parsley, garlic, salt, and pepper thoroughly. Spread the leaves of the artichokes apart. Fill with the bread crumb mixture.

3. Place the artichokes upright in a saucepan to fit snugly. Pour 1 tablespoon of the olive oil over each artichoke. Add water halfway up the artichokes and cover tightly. Cook at low heat for about 45 minutes, or until the artichokes are tender, adding water as necessary. Test by inserting a fork into center of an artichoke. If the heart seems tender to the touch, the artichokes are done. Serve hot or at room temperature.

NOTE   Bread crumbs may be toasted in a toaster oven using the top brown setting two or three times and tossing with a wooden spoon until brown, or by sautéeing in 1 tablespoon of olive oil in a non-stick skillet, tossing constantly with a wooden spoon until brown.

Asparagi alla Parmigiana

•

Asparagus
Baked with
Parmesan
Cheese

6 servings

• Very simple to prepare, this side dish has a rich flavor because of the melted cheese and the hint of freshly ground nutmeg. Fresh fennel wedges can be prepared in the same way. *Parmigiano-Reggiano* is the best choice for cheese when making this recipe.

2 pounds of fresh asparagus spears, bottoms snapped off,
    spears scraped with a vegetable peeler, and rinsed well
6 tablespoons of butter
$^1/_2$ cup of freshly grated Parmesan cheese, or more to taste
freshly grated nutmeg

1. Preheat the oven to 400 degrees.
2. If you are using an asparagus cooker, fill it halfway with lightly salted water and bring to a boil. Stand the asparagus spears in the pot with tips up. Bring back to a boil, cover, and lower the heat to a simmer. Cook until just fork-tender (about 8 minutes). Asparagus may also be cooked, covered, in a large skillet in lightly salted boiling water for 8 minutes or until crisp-tender. Drain the asparagus.
3. Melt half the butter in a baking dish, and place the asparagus lengthwise in the dish. Dot with the remaining butter, and sprinkle with Parmesan and a few grindings of fresh nutmeg.
4. Bake for about 7 minutes, or until the top forms a light golden crust.

192

Dolci

RECIPES

- ### Frutta Fresca con Zabaglione all'Arancia
  FRESH FRUIT WITH ORANGE-ZABAGLIONE CREAM

- ### Sorbetto al Limone
  LEMON SORBET

- ### Pesche al Forno
  PEACHES BAKED WITH AMARETTI FILLING

- ### Biscotti di Mamma
  MOM'S TWICE-BAKED ALMOND BISCOTTI

- ### Brutti ma Buoni
  "UGLY BUT GOOD" CHOCOLATE-HAZELNUT MERINGUE COOKIES

- ### Cucidati
  SICILIAN FIG AND NUT COOKIES

- ### Mele in Crosta
  APPLES IN PUFF PASTRY

- ### Pizzelle con Fragole e Panna
  PIZZELLE WAFER CUPS FILLED WITH STRAWBERRIES AND
  GRAND MARNIER WHIPPED CREAM

- ### Sfinge di San Giuseppe
  ST. JOSEPH'S DAY PASTRIES

ITALY IS KNOWN FOR her many wonderful desserts, made with fresh and dried fruits and nuts. Her pastries are enticing, beautifully displayed in the glass cases of the *pasticcerie* (pastry shops) and coffee bars. On the cooking tours which I lead to all regions of Italy, we look forward to our daily dessert treats: *sfogliatelle*, layers of flaky pastry forming sea-shell shapes and filled with a warm custard; *profiteroles*, small cream-puffs with lemon-cream or chocolate filling; *cannoli*, crispy pastry tubes filled with creamy ricotta, chocolate, and citron; or *mele in crosta*, apples baked in a casing of puff-pastry. The list goes on and on. In addition to individual pastries, there are rich cakes, such as our family's *Cassata alla Siciliana*—a layered sponge cake filled with whipped cream and ricotta and, in Sicily, encased in a marzipan coating. The famous *Pastiera*, or Easter grain pie, is always present in the Naples-Amalfi coast area. *Torte* and *crostate di frutta* (tarts and fruit pies) abound in all of the regions of the country.

Many of the most famous desserts that we continue to make here in America correspond to the feasts of the Catholic Church. One example is the *Sfinge di San Giuseppe*—large pastry puffs baked in the oven and filled with ricotta, chocolate, and candied orange peel. I remember that my Grandpa Tony always served *Zepolle* on that special day as well, (his wife, my grandmother, was named Giuseppina). Those special round pastries were deep-fried and filled with a creamy custard, and crowned with a cherry.

Two years ago, I was scheduled to arrive in Amalfi with a group, to attend the cooking program at the Luna Convento Hotel. I sent a fax to my good friend, Chef Enrico Franzese, and asked him to surprise my friends with the special St. Joseph's pastries for their welcome dinner. We arrived in beautiful Amalfi on the sea, just in time to see the traditional St. Joseph's Day procession, which takes place each year at dusk in front of the awe-inspiring cathedral of St. Andrew in the main square. It moved me to tears to be so far from home yet so close to the traditions that my grandparents had handed down to me when I was a child. The pastries that night had special significance for me!

Most nights, fresh fruit is the simple dessert served after the family dinner. In this chapter, I have included a few recipes that are special in our family. There are three delicious cookie recipes that my mother taught me to make to keep our Italian traditions alive. Her Twice-Baked Almond Biscotti (page 200) are my favorites. I have tried several variations of this recipe, found in many of the new cookbooks that are written only on *biscotti*, but in my opinion, hers are simply the best! The *Brutti ma Buoni*, Ugly But Good Chocolate Meringues (page 202), are a little tricky to make, but they are fabulous.

Finally, the *Cucidati* (page 204), fig-and-nut cookies that we make only at Christmas time, are filled with goodies—and with memories! I first made them when my daughter, Frances, was in kindergarten, 20 years ago. She came home from school one day and announced that she had volunteered to bring in a dish that was "really Italian"—and that did not mean spaghetti and meatballs, which everyone knew how to make! So I hunted through my Italian cookbooks and found a recipe for *Cucidati* in Anna Muffaletto's *The Art of Sicilian Cooking*. After making several dozen, I realized how very labor-intensive they were; I decided to withhold a dozen or so and freeze them for my mother and her sisters, who were coming to Virginia from New York to celebrate Christmas.

On Christmas Eve, after our multi-course seafood extravaganza, out came the *Cassata* and the usual varieties of homemade Christmas cookies. When I presented the *Cucidati*, my mother and aunts began to cry. No one in the family had made these traditional cookies since my grandparents' deaths several years before. Needless to say, Mom and I made them together every Christmas thereafter, until her death in 1993. My daughter, Fran, now makes them with me in the hope that these wonderful traditions will continue into the next generation of Sicilian-Americans in our family.

• This dessert is traditionally made with dry Marsala, a sweet, Sicilian dessert wine, and eaten warm by itself like a custard. In America, it is often served as a sauce over fruit or added to more complicated desserts as part of the filling. This version is particularly refreshing after a rich entrée.

4 egg yolks
$^1/_4$ cup of sugar
$^1/_4$ cup of Grand Marnier or dry Marsala
3 large oranges, peeled, sliced, and halved
1 quart of cleaned fresh strawberries (raspberries and blueberries
    may be substituted or mixed with strawberries)

1. Bring 4 cups of water to simmer in the bottom of a double boiler. Off the heat put the egg yolks in the top of the double boiler and gradually beat in the sugar, using a whisk or electric beater. Add the Grand Marnier, and whisk until blended.
2. Place the yolk mixture over simmering water, being careful that water does not touch the bottom of the pan.
3. Whisk or beat at high speed for 4 to 6 minutes, or until the mixture thickens and its volume increases.
4. Arrange the slices of orange on each individual dessert plate. Top with berries, and spoon warm *zabaglione* cream over the top.

Frutta Fresca con Zabaglione all'Arancia

•

Fresh Fruit with Orange Zabaglione Cream

6 servings

Sorbetto al Limone

• When I was a schoolgirl, I looked forward to savoring an Italian ice at a nearby bakery between the buses I took to get home. Years later, I would enjoy a delicious lemon ice on the Amalfi coast in Italy. Nostalgia is one of the key ingredients in this recipe!

Lemon Sorbet

6 servings

1 ½ cups of sugar
1 ½ cups boiling water
1 tablespoon of grated lemon zest
1 ½ cups of fresh lemon juice
fresh mint leaves for garnish

1. Make a syrup by dissolving the sugar in boiling water, stirring for about 3 minutes. Let the syrup cool slightly, then refrigerate until cold.
2. Combine the syrup, lemon juice, and lemon zest. Pour the mixture into a 9-inch loaf pan. Freeze until solid—several hours or overnight.
3. Break the frozen mixture into chunks, and puree it in a food processor until smooth and creamy. Serve immediately topped with mint leaves, or pack it into a covered container and freeze it for up to 2 days.

ALTERNATIVE METHOD AFTER STEP 2:

Put the mixture into an ice-cream maker, and turn it until you reach the desired consistency.

• This recipe is delicious and quite easy to prepare since the peaches do not have to be peeled before baking. The *Amaretti* cookies called for in the recipe can be found in Italian specialty shops.

6 large, firm, ripe peaches
1/2 cup of sugar
1/2 cup of sliced almonds
6 large or 12 small *Amaretto di Saronno* cookies
1 egg yolk
1/3 cup of *Amaretto di Saronno* liqueur
whipped cream (optional)

1. Preheat the oven to 350 degrees. Butter a large shallow baking dish. Wash and dry the peaches and cut them into halves. Remove the pits and scoop out not more than 1 tablespoon of pulp from each half.
2. In a blender or food processor fitted with a metal blade, combine the peach pulp, sugar, almonds, almond cookies, egg yolk, and liqueur. Blend to a paste.
3. Arrange the peach halves in a single layer in the baking dish, cut side up. Divide the peach-paste mixture among the peach halves. Bake for 20 to 25 minutes.
4. Serve warm or at room temperature. Top with whipped cream, if desired.

Pesche al Forno

•

Peaches Baked with Amaretti Filling

12 servings

Biscotti di Mamma

●

Mom's Twice-Baked Almond Biscotti

Three dozen biscotti

● These *biscotti* are favorites all over Italy. In Tuscany, they are called *Biscotti di Prati* and are dipped in a sweet dessert wine called *Vin Santo*. My Mom's recipe uses pure anise oil, which can be found in Italian specialty markets or ordered from your local pharmacist. It is very expensive, but it lasts a long time as it is used sparingly. The cookies are baked, sprinkled with sugar and cinnamon, and baked again on both sides, which produces very crispy *biscotti*. Enjoy!

3 eggs, well beaten
1 cup of sugar
$1/2$ cup of vegetable oil
1 teaspoon of anise oil (anise extract may be substituted, or
    other flavorings, such as almond or vanilla, may be used)
1 tablespoon of grated orange rind
1 teaspoon of grated lemon rind
2 tablespoons of orange juice
3 cups of flour, plus a little extra
$1/4$ teaspoon of salt
3 teaspoons of baking powder
1 cup sliced or coarsely chopped almonds, toasted
1 teaspoon of cinnamon
2 tablespoons sugar

1. In a large mixing bowl, beat the eggs until thick and lemon-colored.
2. Add 1 cup of sugar very gradually, beating constantly.
3. Add the oil, flavorings, lemon and orange rinds, and orange juice.

4. In a separate bowl, mix the flour, salt, baking powder, and nuts together. Add this mixture one third at a time to the egg mixture to form a soft dough. The dough will be sticky.

15. Chill the dough in its bowl for 15 minutes in the freezer or 1 hour in the refrigerator. (Alternatively, you may form and bake it immediately but the dough will be more difficult to handle.)

16. Preheat the oven to 350 degrees.

17. Divide the dough into three parts. Dip your hands in flour and knead the dough into a long strip, 1-inch thick and 10 to 12-inches long. Place on a greased baking sheet. Pat the strip to make it slightly flat. Use the rest of the dough to make two more strips. For larger *biscotti*, form only two strips.

18. Bake for 35 minutes.

19. Remove from the oven and slice the strips on the diagonal while hot. Lay the slices flat on a cookie sheet. Turn the oven down to 275 degrees.

10. Mix together the cinnamon and 2 tablespoons of sugar. Sprinkle the cinnamon-sugar mixture on the *biscotti*, and toast in the oven for 10 minutes on each side. Store the *biscotti* in tins.

Brutti ma

Buoni

•

*"Ugly But
Good"
Chocolate-
Hazelnut
Meringue
Cookies*

*Approximately
36 meringue
cookies*

• These unique cookies, which are yummy but not very pretty to look at, are a little bit tricky to make. My mother had been making these for years when I decided to try them on my own. The first few attempts were not too successful until I watched her make them one day.

I pass on these few tips to you. Always weigh the ingredients. The amounts of confectioner's sugar and nuts must be equal. Add the egg whites slowly; sometimes it is necessary to use less egg white, sometimes more. Work the whites into the dry ingredients with a wooden spoon just until the whites hold the mixture together. The batter should not be runny or overly moist, or the meringues will spread out too much and not puff up as they should. Be sure to wet your hands before forming the balls of dough; this will help with the stickiness of the batter. And always use parchment paper to line the cookie sheets, as the meringues will lift off easily when cool. *Buona fortuna* (good luck)!

1 pound of hazelnuts, roasted and skinned
parchment paper
1 pound of confectioner's sugar
4 tablespoons of unsweetened cocoa
1 teaspoon of cinnamon
3 egg whites (or 4, if small), at room temperature

1. Preheat the oven to 375 degrees. Roast the hazelnuts on a cookie sheet or perforated pizza pan for 15 minutes. Wrap the nuts in a clean cotton kitchen towel, and roll back and forth on the kitchen counter to release the skins from the nuts. Discard the skins.
2. Lower the oven temperature to 325 degrees. Line two large baking sheets with parchment paper.

3. Put the hazelnuts in the bowl of a food processor and give 4 to 5 quick pulses, or pound the nuts with a mallet to crush them coarsely. Some of the nuts should remain whole or in large pieces.
4. In a large bowl, mix the sugar, cocoa, cinnamon, and nuts. Add the egg whites slowly, mixing with a wooden spoon or spatula until all the ingredients are just moistened.
5. With wet hands, roll the dough into 1 1/2-inch balls, drop them onto the prepared cookie sheets, and bake them for 25 minutes. Check to see if the meringues are too soft in the center. If so, bake 5 to 10 minutes more.
6. Remove the meringues from the oven and let them stand for 5 to 10 minutes before peeling off the parchment and transferring them to a plate or tin. The meringues can be stored in tins for two weeks or frozen in plastic containers.

NOTE   This recipe can easily be halved.

Cucidati

•

*Sicilian Fig
and Nut
Cookies*

*5 dozen
cookies*

• Every year when my Mom and I got together to begin our Christmas baking, she would retell the story of how these cookies were made when she was a little girl, long before there were electric food processors. Her mother, aunts, and cousins would gather to hand-chop the figs, nuts, dates, and orange peel, and to painstakingly measure out all of the dry ingredients. Everyone would help form, bake, and decorate the *cucidati*, and when they were all done, they were stored in large tins or cloth sacks, to be divided among the various families when Christmas arrived.

They were indeed a labor of love, and no Christmas Eve celebration would be complete without them, even today. Just ask my youngest sister, Jo Ellen, who expects a platter of them every year no matter where we gather for *La Vigilia*!

FILLING:

12 ounces of dried figs
4 ounces of dates or dark Dakota figs
1 cup of golden sultana raisins
the rind of 1 large orange
1/2 pound of almond or hazelnut meats (or a mixture of both),
    roasted and chopped
1 cup of honey
1/2 cup of bourbon whiskey
1 teaspoon of cinnamon
a pinch of nutmeg
1/4 cup of apricot preserves (optional)

PASTRY DOUGH:

2 1/2 cups of pre-sifted flour
1/2 cup of sugar
2 1/2 teaspoons of baking powder
1/4 teaspoon of salt
1/2 cup of butter or margarine
2 eggs
1/2 teaspoon of vanilla
1/4 cup of milk

ICING:

1 1/2 cups of confectioner's sugar
the juice of 2 small lemons
multicolored cake-decorating sprinkles

1. Preheat the oven to 400 degrees.
2. In a food processor, grind the figs, dates, raisins, orange rind, and nuts together until a coarse mixture is formed. Transfer to a 3-quart saucepan.
3. Stir in the honey, bourbon, cinnamon, nutmeg, and apricot preserves (if desired). Simmer on low heat for 5 to 7 minutes, stirring well. Let cool completely.
4. In a medium bowl, sift the flour, sugar, baking powder, and salt together. Cut in the butter or margarine with a pastry blender or two knives, until the mixture resembles coarse cornmeal. Stir in the eggs, vanilla, and milk until the dough can be gathered up with your fingers to form a ball. Finish kneading by hand. (This procedure may also be done in a food processor). Divide the dough into 4 parts, wrap each part in plastic wrap, and refrigerate for at least 1 hour.
5. Remove 1/4 of the dough at a time, and roll it out 1/4-inch thick on a floured

board. Cut into 4-inch strips. Spread a row of filling 1-inch thick on the lower half of one strip. Fold the top half of the dough over to cover the filling. With fingers or a fork, press the edges together to seal in the filling. Cut the filled strip on the diagonal into 1 to 2-inch pieces. Slash each piece on top once with a sharp knife. Repeat until all the dough is used up. Remove another $1/4$ of the dough from the refrigerator, and continue as above until the remaining dough is used up. If there is filling left over, it can be frozen for future use.

6. Grease two large baking sheets. Place the cookie slices on the baking sheets 1 inch apart, and bake until lightly browned (about 15 to 20 minutes). Remove from the oven and cool on wire racks that have waxed paper underneath.

7. In a small bowl, combine the confectioner's sugar with the juice. Glaze the cookies with icing, and immediately decorate with sprinkles.

NOTE   Cookies may also be made in the shape of wreaths by wrapping each strip of filled dough into a circle before baking. Dough wreaths should be slashed on top with a sharp knife in several places before baking.

• Chef Enrico made this beautiful, delicious dessert at the Luna Convento Cooking School in Amalfi. He made his puff-pastry from scratch—a very long process. I find the results when using frozen puff pastry sheets to be very satisfactory.

  1 sheet of frozen puff pastry
  4 apples
  5 ounces of apricot jam, plus extra for glaze if desired
  1 egg plus 1 tablespoon water, lightly beaten for egg wash
  parchment paper

1. Preheat the oven to 375 degrees. Remove the sheet of pastry from the freezer to soften for 30 minutes.
2. Peel the apples thoroughly and remove the cores.
3. Fill the cavity of each apple with jam.
4. Line the jelly roll pan with parchment paper.
5. Roll out the pastry and cut into 4 square pieces, leaving enough extra to top each apple with a small pastry square or round.
6. Wrap each square around 1 apple by lifting the corners and joining them in the center with a twist. Cover the top with a piece of pastry.
7. Brush the pastries with the egg wash. Place them on a baking pan lined with parchment paper.
8. Bake for 35 to 40 minutes, or until puffed and golden.

OPTIONAL TOUCH:

When the pastries have cooled, brush them with additional apricot jam that has been boiled with a little water until the jam melts, about 3 to 4 minutes.

Pizzelle con Fragole e Panna

Pizzelle Wafer Cups Filled with Strawberries and Grand Marnier Whipped Cream

5 1/2 dozen flat pizzelles

• *Pizzelle* are light, crispy, waffle-like cookies from the Abruzzi region of Italy. They must be pressed in a special iron similar to a waffle iron. Electric *Pizzelle* irons can be purchased at kitchen shops, and in some Italian specialty food markets. My *pizzelle* iron is 20 years old, and shows the caramelizing effect of the thousands of *pizzelle* it has pressed out. In this recipe, I form cups from the *pizzelle* and fill them with fresh strawberries and cream. In winter, I fill them with ice cream and dark cherries with a jubilee sauce. A very elegant dessert.

BATTER FOR THE PIZZELLE:

12 eggs
2 cups of sugar
2 cups of vegetable oil
2 teaspoons of pure lemon *or* pure orange extract
1/2 teaspoon of pure anise oil (you may substitute
    1 tablespoon of anise extract)
4 cups of flour (2 cups of all-purpose flour plus 2 cups
    of cake flour, such as Swan's Down)

FILLING:

2 quarts of cleaned strawberries, halved
2 cups of heavy whipping cream
1/2 to 3/4 cup of confectioner's sugar
2 tablespoons of Grand Marnier (or to taste)

1. Beat the eggs well, until lemon-colored, adding the sugar gradually.
2. Add the oil and flavorings, and beat until smooth.
3. Add the flour a little at a time, and beat until well blended.

4. Let the batter stand for at least 1 hour, or chill overnight to enrich the flavor. Bring the batter to room temperature.
5. Heat the *pizzelle* iron until hot. Brush with a little vegetable oil to prevent sticking. Put enough batter on each side of the iron to cover the small inner circle. Close the top and press down for a few seconds to make the *pizzelle* thin. This will insure a crisp wafer when cooled. When golden brown, remove the *pizzelle* from the iron. While it is still warm and pliable, place it in a small fluted dessert dish and let it cool until hardened. Repeat this until all the batter is used. To store the *pizzelle* put them in a large airtight tin.
6. To serve, fill the *pizzelle* cups with fresh strawberries and whipped cream that has been sweetened with sugar and Grand Marnier to taste.

NOTE   *Pizzelle* may be served flat as a cookie sprinkled with confectioner's sugar, instead of forming them in dessert cups.

Sfinge di San Giuseppe

*

St. Joseph's Day Pastries

24 puffs

• These special ricotta-filled pastry puffs are found both in the United States and in Italy every year during the two-week period before and after the feast of St. Joseph, on March 19. In this version the puffs are baked, but I have often tasted them deep-fried before filling. Both ways are absolutely delicious.

FILLING:

2 pounds of ricotta, drained in a colander for 10 minutes
3/4 cup of confectioner's sugar, or more to taste
1/3 cup of chocolate-covered orange peel, diced *or*
    2 tablespoons of chopped candied orange and
    3 tablespoons of chopped bittersweet chocolate

PASTRY PUFFS:

1/2 cup of unsalted butter (1 stick)
1 cup of flour
a pinch of salt
4 eggs, at room temperature
1 1/2 tablespoons of sugar
1/2 teaspoon of lemon rind, grated
1 1/2 tablespoons of vanilla
parchment paper

1. Prepare the filling by pulsing the ricotta in a food processor with the confectioner's sugar until smooth, or by beating with an electric mixer. Fold in the chocolate and orange peel. Refrigerate.

2. In a medium saucepan, bring 1 cup of water and the butter to a boil over medium-high heat. Take the pan off the burner and add the flour and a pinch of salt all at once. Stir vigorously with a wooden spoon, putting the pan back on the heat. The mixture will become pasty and form a ball in about 30 seconds. Turn the paste into a medium bowl and let cool.
3. Preheat the oven to 425 degrees.
4. Beat the dough with an electric mixer, adding the eggs one at a time, being careful to mix thoroughly before adding the next egg. The dough will become soft and smooth. Add the sugar, lemon rind, and vanilla.
5. Drop by tablespoonsful onto a baking sheet lined with parchment paper, leaving at least 2 inches between. Bake for 15 minutes, then lower the heat to 325 degrees and continue baking for 20 minutes or until puffed and golden.
6. Remove the pastry puffs from the oven, let them stand for 10 minutes, and slice off the top third. With a fork, remove any wet batter from inside the puffs, and fill them with the ricotta filling. Arrange the pastry puffs on a serving platter. They may be refrigerated up to 2 hours. Dust the tops with confectioner's sugar before serving.

TIP   The puffs may be frozen, unfilled, after cooling, and then crisped in a 375-degree oven for 10 minutes before filling.

Raffaello, Chef Walter, and Cathie Sur
Kitchen at Montinope, Abruzzo

Agata & Valentina
1505 First Avenue at 79th Street • New York, NY
(212) 452-0690 • Fax: (212) 452-0694

Fresh, seasonal organic produce; fresh pasta and mozzarella; brick-oven pizza and *focaccia*; extra-virgin olive oils and Sicilian organic olive oil. Many other Sicilian specialties, including *arancine, caponata,* salted sardines and anchovies, *estratto di pomodoro,* and capers.

Mike & Son's Delicatessen
Arthur Avenue Retail Market
(David Grecco)
2344 Arthur Avenue • New York, NY 10458
(718) 295-5033

Excellent variety of cheeses: *Parmigiano-Reggiano,* fresh mozzarella, provolone, imported Prosciutto di Parma, sopressata, *focaccia, arancine,* and olives.
Will Ship

Addeo Bakers, Inc.
(Larry and Sal)
2352 Arthur Avenue • Bronx, NY 10458
(718) 367-8316

All varieties of Italian bread and hand-rolled breadsticks.
Will Ship

Gilbertie's Herb Garden, Inc.
7 Sylvan Lane • Westport, CT 06880
(203) 227-4175

Grows more than 400 varieties of herb plants, as well as rare vegetable plants, and sells a variety of herb products at the Westport store and nationwide.

Mt. Carmel Gourmet Food Shop
Arthur Avenue Retail Market
2344 Arthur Avenue • Bronx, NY 10458

Excellent selection of extra-virgin olive oils and handmade dried pastas, as well as other Italian specialty foods.

SOUTHWEST

Paula Lambert's Mozzarella Company
2944 Elm Street • Dallas, TX 75226
1-800-798-2954 • Fax: (214) 741-4076

Fresh mozzarella, *Mozzarella di Bufala,* ricotta, *Mascarpone,* goat cheese and *caciotta.*
Will Ship

WEST COAST

Manicaretti
5332 College Avenue, Suite 200 • Oakland, CA 94618
1-800-799-9830
(Call for the retail location nearest you).

Excellent selection of extra-virgin olive oils and super fino rice (arborio, carnaroli), handcrafted dried pasta, and farro (whole and crushed).

Index